IDENTITY
SHIFT

ISBN: 978-19-5-315340-1

Published by

LIFESTYLE ENTREPRENEURS PRESS

If you are interested in publishing through Lifestyle Entrepreneurs Press, write to: Publishing@LifestyleEntrepreneursPress.com

Publications or foreign rights acquisition of our catalog books.
Learn More: www.LifestyleEntrepreneursPress.com

Printed in the USA

IDENTITY
SHIFT

UPGRADE HOW YOU OPERATE
TO ELEVATE YOUR LIFE

ANTHONY TRUCKS

To my incredible wife.
You're more amazing than I can put into words.
Even though half the time I want to punch you
in the face. With my lips ;-)

YOU'VE GOT THE BOOK, NOW GRAB YOUR BONUSES.

Resources   **Workbook**   **Audiobook**   **Digital Book**

Head to **www.IdentityShiftBook.com/resources** and use code **BOOKBONUSES**

Contents

PART 1

THE CREATION

PROLOGUE

3:33 a.m.... Three more hours until I have to get up. Ugh. It's Tuesday, and I can feel the impending doom of having to get up and start another week.

Why can't I just sit here and let the world press on for a minute? Not going to lie, I envy homeless people just a little bit because they don't have to worry about going through the daily motions to keep the bills paid.

When's my next vacation?

Crap it's 3:54 a.m. TURN OFF, BRAIN! I need to get back to sleep.

Well, now I'm anxious, and my heart's beating all fast, and I don't know how I'm going to fall back...

BEEP BEEP BEEP BEEP... *6:30 a.m. already?!*

OK, Ken. Get up. Seriously, get up. You have to be at that meeting by 7:00 a.m. and you cannot skip brushing your teeth again just because you want to get some more sleep.

One foot; great job. Second foot; there you go. Now stand up. Yes, I'm proud of you, man. Now head to the bathroom and get going. Shower?

Sniff... *Naw, you're good for now. Teeth?* "Hawh..." *Yes, teeth, you dummy. That's gross. Clothes? These blue jeans, and that wrinkled yellow shirt on the ground, and those white chucks look wearable.*

Annnnnd we're dressed and ready to... Oh crap! I'm late!

OK, you're out the door and you're on your way to the coffee shop. You'll get there soon.

Why do you always do this, man? You give yourself anxiety every day for what?

I don't know, and I don't feel like thinking about it right now.

I wonder what's going on in Facebook land. Ding! "Hey, Ken, how's that book coming along? Also, are you still going to launch that business you talked about, or apply for that job you mentioned?"

Hmmmm... Going to ignore that one for now. I don't feel like getting into that conversation at the moment. I'll come up with an excuse later so I don't have to admit I'm all over the place and I don't know when I'm going to get any of that stuff done because every time I set a deadline, it passes before I even get started.

I don't know what it is with me. I'm talented, passionate, motivated (most of the time), and I know what needs to be done, but I'm stuck in a standstill, saying the same things month after month.

What the F$#!!* "Learn to drive, you idiot! I can't STAND it when people cut me off!"

Man, if I didn't have somewhere to be, I'd give him a piece of my mind. That's going to be under my skin for hours. People really piss me off!

Jeez, late. Again. It's OK, though. Christine knows I'm always a little bit late, and she's a close friend, so I'm sure she'll understand and let me off the hook.

As I rounded the corner, there was Christine, looking as healthy as ever, with a pretty white and blue flowered dress, fishing around in her medium-sized brown bag. Her cup of coffee was almost finished, and as she peeked up through her curls, which sat at shoulder height, she finally saw me. Her scrunched-up face said more than any words could have.

"What's up, Christine? How are you? Some idiot on the way here cut me off."

"You know what, Ken? Honestly, I'm a little bothered that you're 10 minutes late and didn't even text me to let me know you were running late. I figured you respected me enough to show up on time or at least let me know."

"I'm sorry, I...uh...ran into some traffic on the way here. Somebody cut me off, and I couldn't find a parking spot. It's not a disrespect thing."

"Well, I got here 10 minutes early, so I've been waiting here for 20 minutes already. Honestly, I wouldn't have even mentioned it, but it's become a pattern. Even though we've been friends for over 10 years, I don't have space in my life for people who operate like you, Ken."

"Wait, what do you mean? Are you serious right now? All this because I'm 10 minutes late?!"

"It's way deeper than that, and you know it. We talked about this the last time you did this to me. We both started our careers at the same time, and we were pretty equal back then, but I chose over the last few years to make some adjustments to my life, and you haven't. To be totally honest, I love you, but you need to figure some things out in life or I'm going to have to love you from a distance."

"You've got to be kidding me right now. What makes you so special?! You think you're better than me just because you make more money and have achieved some stuff. I could do the exact same things you are, dammit!"

"Better than you? What are you talking about? Do you really want to do this right now? If you do, I'll break it down for you because the only person between the two of us who thinks that might be you. What you do with what I have to say is up to you, but I'm telling you right now, it's going to hurt to hear."

"Hurt me? Why would you want to hurt me? What's gotten into you?! This is ridiculous. You're nobody special!"

Then Christine gave me a look I didn't expect after calling her a nobody in public. She looked me deep in the eyes with the most caring expression I've ever seen a person place in my direction and calmly said something I'll never forget. "You know my heart, Ken. I've always tried to help you, but I cannot help you if you're unwilling to help yourself. I can't want more for you than you want for yourself, and right now, I want you to have the most incredible life, but you're the one who doesn't."

What does she mean I don't want an incredible life? Of course I do. Am I being punked right now?

"It's clear in the way you operate every day of your life. It's who you are to be late, lazy, lethargic, and make excuses. You're always talking about the things you're going to do, and you never follow through, then you talk down about people who do. If this is who you're committed to being, then I can't be committed to being in your life."

My heart sunk, and all I could do was swallow with a dumbfounded look on my face as I stared back at her for what felt like 10 minutes.

"Ken, it's only a matter of time before everyone else tells you the same, or doesn't and just avoids you. I'm telling you this BECAUSE I love you enough to tell you what you need to hear, not what you want to hear. If you want to sit down, and calm down, I'll let you in on what my heart believes your heart needs to hear."

I took a moment to gather my thoughts, still a little pissed off from the drive over and this conversation. Then, I reluctantly and anxiously sat down with crossed arms and a standoffish feeling, knowing that I was about to hear something that may hurt and help me at the same time. Just like getting a shot from the doctor—you know it's going to hurt, but deep down you know you need it to get healthy.

"I'm all ears, Christine," I said with just the slightest sarcasm in my voice.

She shrugged it off and went in. The hours seemed to slide by as she cancelled her upcoming appointments and laid into me with the toughest love I'd ever experienced. I wanted to punch her and hug her at the same time.

What she shared opened my mind to something I'd never noticed, and, in fact, it was crystal clear why she'd had so much more success than me in such a short time, even though I had access to the same people, information, time, and had the same capabilities.

The secret was hidden in what she did over the last 24 hours.

"Look, Ken, there's nothing wrong with you, but there is something wrong with how you operate, and it's not even your fault. People who are stuck at the start, and even multi-millionaires who feel like there's something missing, need the same thing to get to their next level.

"A few years back, I happened across a concept that's literally changed my entire life. I know I'm going to sound like some self-help infomercial, but I'm telling you it's impacted every single part of my life, and I only wish I'd found it, and mentioned it to you, earlier.

"In fact, the only reason we're friends now is because I met you before I knew this, and right now, if I'd just met you, I wouldn't give you the time of day, not because of who you are but because of how you operate in life. What I'm going to share is a simple but powerful way to elevate all areas of your life."

Wow. Talk about a gut punch. She wouldn't even be my friend if she'd just met me. I REALLY hope this is going somewhere good because I'm about to get up and walk out of here.

"First, let me tell you a little story, and then I'll tell you what 95 percent of people miss in the story that separates them from success.

"Five years ago, I used to hate getting up on Mondays because I knew I wasn't getting up to do anything I enjoyed. I dreaded counting the time down on my alarm clock, and I hated the sound of my alarm even more because I knew it was forcing me into a day I wasn't looking forward to. Like you probably are now, I was always slow to get up and get going, so I'd also be late and make excuses for it every time.

Dang, she's describing my life to a tee. I can't let her know that just yet though.

"I don't know if this is you also, but I used to have these big ideas, dreams, and goals. I would tell everyone what I was going to do, and I was super excited, but nothing ever got going. Then I'd make a bunch of excuses about what happened, even though, in my quiet, dark moments, I knew I was making excuses that sounded good but weren't accurate."

Christine was reading me like a damn book right now. I couldn't even muster up words to respond as my head slowly began to shake in agreeance to what she was saying.

She continued. "So, I'd get overwhelmed, stressed, frustrated, and procrastinate until I made a good excuse to move on to something else. Excuses that were usually ways to get through the day without feeling bad about myself. The excuses were for things that I knew in my heart were unacceptable, like being late to meetings and expecting people to just let me slide.

"Whenever things in life would go wrong or something unexpected would happen, I'd let it get to me, and it would stick in my gut as anger, for the entire day sometimes. I gave people, and the world, the keys to drive me crazy. I was like a leaf in the wind without any real direction or discipline, and as much as I knew it wasn't OK, I kept lying to myself and saying it was OK.

"Then, I was watching everyone around me having more and achieving more. I would tear them down and/or make up reasons that they were doing better than me that were based on luck or timing so I didn't have to accept that I needed to be and do better. It was easier that way, instead of being real with myself about the truth.

"The truth is that I had the information, I knew what needed to be done, I knew how to do it, but I couldn't get out of my own way. I was the biggest obstacle I was facing because I had every other thing I needed to succeed, or at least had access to it."

She was right, and I was finally beginning to realize that not only did she get it, and me, but she was actually heading in a direction that could probably help me. I just needed to keep biting my tongue. I wanted to say so many things, but all I could muster was, "What did you find out then?"

"Let me finish the story, and I'll get to that.

"I had this exact conversation with someone I cared about when I showed up late for the third time in a row. So, believe me when

I say I know EXACTLY how you feel right this second. It's like someone is sticking a stir rod into your stomach; they're mixing your emotions up like some uncomfortable emotional soup."

"Well, you hit that on the head, Christine. I don't even know what to do with this right now. I was hoping to get a scone and a coffee then chill, and now I want to curl up and die," I said with a smirk and a light chuckle.

That lifted the energy enough, and I could see her tension shrink, which lowered mine, and she continued her story. "Before I tell you exactly what he said, I want you to know how the last 24 hours have gone for me. I got up at 5:00 a.m. yesterday and did a 30-minute workout followed by a 15-minute meditation. When I got out of the shower, around 6:00 a.m., I was feeling amazing and had joy in me when I was making breakfast. I texted my fiancé that I was excited to have lunch with him later, and my heart swelled, knowing that was going to be a great break from the work I was doing. Work I'm enjoying doing, I must say.

"Then I got an email that could have thrown off my entire Monday morning. My stomach sank into the floor, and I could feel my emotions twist up like a Twizzler. I wanted to freak out and be angry the entire day, but instead, I did what I've been doing for years now: I managed the emotion in a way that didn't allow me to carry it and ruin the rest of my day. That isn't who I am anymore.

"I kept my schedule and realized I couldn't do anything about it right this second. I pressed on and did it with joy still in me. I wasn't burying it or faking it; just not letting it control me. I was off to my workspace to get the week started off right.

All I could think was: *Shoot, Christine. Can you teach me?*

"About a mile from my home, someone ran a red light and almost hit me. I was pissed and wanted to scream. I did, actually, but I also took a second to think about what kind of emotional place that person must be in to feel they needed to do that, and it dawned on me that they were probably in an anxious rush, and I wasn't about to let their bad day rub off on me. I'm not that kind of person anymore. So, I released it and headed into work."

How in the world is she able to do this? The more she talks the more I want to know how this is all possible.

"I arrived at work with a lightness to me, and no one would have known about the two things that had already happened because I had the right response tactics in place to ground me and to navigate those moments. That's who I am now.

"I went to my desk and was happy to look at my calendar because I clearly realized that I had nothing lingering. I was completely up to speed with all my projects. Some finished and some in progress. Even the unfinished ones had been placed into my life with a strategy that allows me to have open loops with zero stress because I know I'm making proper progress."

I was still listening but wondering when she was going to get to the point because at this point, I just felt like she was rubbing things in my face. I kept quiet and let her continue.

"Then I got a call that my fiancé had a project to finish and had to cancel lunch. It bothered me, but instead of responding angrily, I let him know it was OK, because it was, and I wasn't mad at all because I know his heart and it must have been serious. That's who I am now. I let him know we'd connect after work.

"I got through my day ahead of schedule on my projects, felt great that I was making progress, and I looked forward to seeing my fiancé that evening. I wasn't even close to any burnout or stress. In fact, I had a thought in the elevator that gave me a wave of pride for a second when I realized that I had gotten so much done without struggle that day, and Kelly had mentioned the week before how easy I made everything look even though I was getting three times more done than her in a week.

"It wasn't an 'I'm better than people' feeling as much as it was an 'I'm better than I was' feeling. I was getting three times more done with three times less stress, anxiety, overwhelm, anger, resentment, or anything remotely close to burnout. I've been able to accomplish so much more in so much less time in comparison to other people, and I owe it all to a simple shift given to me by my friend."

I was on the edge of my seat now. *Who's this friend? What shift is she talking about?*

"Before I was given this same talk, I would have slept in until 6:30 a.m., got up rushing, checked my email, and let the freak-out emotion immediately carry on throughout the rest of my day. I would have texted my fiancé with frustration and might have even started a small fight on accident. Then, I would have rushed breakfast and ran out the door, only to have someone run the red light and leave me feeling red inside.

"Then, I'd show up to work in a bad mood and walk in with my head down. I'd scurry to my desk and plop down in time to see a list of unfinished projects and tasks that would make my blood boil, and I'd get overwhelmed, frustrated, stressed, angry, and helpless. Not to mention I was out of shape and didn't even like the way I looked in the mirror. Then, if my fiancé would have texted to cancel, I would have flown off the handle and started a fight, even though, deep down, I knew he wasn't trying to cause a problem.

"I'd get up to leave work and pass by the work areas of other people doing incredible things and be even more pissed off that they were getting success and I wasn't. My life honestly sucked.

I didn't know what to do, and even if I did, I wouldn't have even felt like doing anything about it, even though I had all the exact same access to information, support, resources, time, and everything I have right now."

At this moment, I realized how intimately Christine knew my situation. For the first time in as long as I could remember, I didn't feel alone.

"There was one singular difference about who I am now and who I was then that has allowed me to make more money, be happier, have more success, and do it all with less stress and anxiety. A difference that my friend finally sat me down and enlightened me on. It was how I was operating in my life."

"Operating, Christine? Did you just tell me that entire story to leave me with some vague statement? I mean, I'm happy for you, but I have no idea what that's even supposed to mean."

"Well, Ken, neither did I. He walked me through a day of his, just like I did to you, and he made it clear why 95 percent of people stay stuck and stressed. Then, he shared how the others make millions of dollars, have happy relationships, are in good shape, get a ton done without stress, and achieve goals in ways that look easy.

"Their lives aren't any easier, and they experience the exact same, if not more, difficulty in life. They simply operate at a level far above the 95 percent, and it's actually in a way that feels effortless. Because of this they do things that seem incredibly difficult for others with a sense of ease. They're slow to anger, are disciplined and consistent, make great positive decisions in emotional moments, have great organizational skills, effective and efficient habits, and a powerful mindset. They take bold action, have strong, optimistic thoughts, and there's a personal pride they carry that allows them to control their lives and themselves in ways that seems so out of reach for people that they're considered 'special.'"

Christine just described a superhero, and although I like comic books, I'm pretty sure a person like that doesn't exist. If they do, then I need to learn how to become one!

"He was clear that it wasn't because he was any smarter than others, didn't have any more time, no more money or important resources, or connections. He was the guy who shouldn't have succeeded on paper but did. It was who he WAS with what he had. It was how he operated with the things he had access to in life that made the difference.

"While everyone was looking for the silver-bullet product and informational edge, he was operating in a way that taught him lessons and garnered him info no one could buy. It gave him confidence no one could shake, a drive no one could slow, which resulted in success no one could understand or match.

"See, Ken, the definition of 'operating' is to control the functions of a machine, process, or system. We're biological machines that are run by an invisible operating system called an identity. This identity is functioning at all times without us even realizing it, but it's controlling the system. That system is our lives.

"The simplest way to think about your identity is that it's who you are and what you do when you are not thinking about who you are or what you're doing. When you're just in flow and not even realizing what you're doing, how you're thinking, how you're reacting, or consciously considering how this moment will affect the next moments of your life.

"People just effortlessly flow through their lives, and that's OK, but the level at which they're operating in that effortless flow is so low and unintentional that the outcomes in their lives are undesirable. So, when people are in that same effortless flow but operating at a peak levels, their outcomes in life are amazing, and it feels just as effortless."

I don't know why, but the wheels are starting to spin. Something somehow is actually starting to make sense.

"What you really need to know is that there are three key stages of operating: how you plan for future moments, how you handle the planned moments when they arrive, and how you handle the unplanned moments. Most people have no clue how to plan to begin with, Ken. Then they arrive at moments unprepared and ruin the moments they did plan, and if anything unexpected happens, it shuts them down, and opportunities pass them by without them even knowing it.

"So, when you start, and experience, your entire day with frustration and poor success, it's because of the mindless program running, your identity, that's operating at a low level. No planning, and no strategy for planned or unplanned moments.

"There are six core drivers of your identity, which are your beliefs, thoughts, big actions, habits, mindset, and ego. These all swim in a social, racial, and cultural pool as well. Your identity is running from those drivers, within those environmental factors, and handling all those moments. Unfortunately, it's doing a bad job. I know because that was me.

"So, when you get unexpected news or have unexpected situations happen, your system starts running and takes you off track without you knowing it. Next thing you know, your core drivers kick into higher gear, but they function poorly, so you get overwhelmed, frustrated, and slide so far behind you don't even want to come back up for air, regardless of how talented, smart, accomplished, or motivated you are. It's not what you know or have access to; it's who you are with what you know and have access to.

"That's when he shared something that blew my mind and brought everything full circle for me. Your identity is how you operate. How you operate determines how you perform in life daily. How you perform consistently, over time, determines the success, or lack thereof, you'll have in life. Your success will ultimately determine whether or not you have success and elevate your life.

"So, identity will determine how great or poor of a life you'll live. If you upgrade how you operate, at an identity level, you'll elevate your life.

"It's the simple golden thread the most successful people in the world share and the unsuccessful struggle to attain."

My head was spinning trying to make sense of all of this. *How in the world am I supposed to think about my identity, and what do I do with this information? Identity has always seemed like some airy psychological concept, and now I'm being told it will make or break my success in life?*

"So, Christine, what exactly are you saying right now? In layman's terms."

"Ken, what I'm saying is that the only reason you're not having the success you and I both know you're capable of is because you suck at operating your life and you need to upgrade how you operate at an identity level.

"Your operation is showing up in how you plan, how you handle planned moments, and how you handle unplanned moments. That's literally where you will make or break everything in your life. Sadly, you won't even notice you've ruined things, and if you do, it'll be far too late to do anything about it.

I thought we were just going to have a coffee and a chat, but I think Christine is about to change my life with this meeting.

"The moment your mind finally understands this will be the day your life starts to elevate like mine and everyone else in the world who has higher levels of success. You shouldn't feel bad, though, because your operating system, your identity, was programmed unintentionally by your environment, without you even knowing, by the time you were in your late teens. Your parents, teachers, teammates, coaches, friends, TV, radio, and even random people in life all passively taught you things, and you adopted those patterns and identity traits that have been running your life all along.

"So, yes, we used to be fairly equal but you're still operating poorly, which turned into performing poorly. So, your ability to succeed died, and your life got stagnant without you knowing why.

"In fact, you just accepted your life as it is, like most people, and you settled into mediocrity as you gave up on trying to achieve more. So you've ended up embracing being a late, lazy, lethargic, and excuse-ridden person."

Shoot. Yep, she pegged me dead on.

"I get it, though, because I used to be you. Why try if nothing will ever change? That's the question that kills all dreams because it's an assumption that you've worked as hard as possible and nothing's changed, or that success is only for special, magical people. It's not. Success is waiting to be achieved by anyone willing to accept that they need to upgrade how they operate and take the actions to make that upgrade into the person, at an identity level, who has all the things they want most in life. Logically, if you were that person, you'd already have those things."

"So you're saying I just need to upgrade how I operate, and everything will get better?"

"Yes. You need to upgrade how you operate, and you will elevate every single area of your life. You can easily do it by making a shift at an identity level through strategic actions and habits, over time, so that one day you barely even notice how well you're doing things in life. It'll feel just as easy and effortless as how you're doing things now though. You'll be getting a ton done, but it will feel effortless because it'll be who you are to get a ton done."

"I think I get what you're saying, Christine, but isn't this just 'mindset' that you're talking about?"

"I wish. You know, I was a college athlete, Ken, so I have a great mindset, but I was still struggling. I asked the same question, actually. That's when he made it incredibly clear that I didn't want to blur that line."

"In fact, he told me that I would be wasting my time on mindset if I didn't focus on identity. I don't randomly take people at their word when they go against the grain like this, so I needed proof. He actually sent me some studies on 'self-categorization,' better known as identity, from George Washington University that clearly showed how people applying mindset tactics alone fell short of success because deep down they fought against the part of them that 'knew' it wasn't who they were to do that new thing.

"Once a new identity is in place, mindset becomes a powerful tool that makes success easier, but without the new identity, mindset work is surface level, and the moment you hit unexpected circumstances and don't have some random tactic to apply, you backslide and fall apart. In these studies, when the participants' actions aligned with who they were at an identity level to handle those moments, their identities kicked in and filled the spaces where their mindsets didn't show up. So they succeeded with ease more often and made it look easy.

Wow, she's breaking down the science of all this. I'm definitely not at her level. And to think I was bothered that she thought she was better than me. She might actually be better... Can't believe I just said that to myself.

"Mindset versus identity is like using two tactics to make a white flower blue. One tactic is to dry and coat the flower in blue paint, like dipping it into blue paint or spray painting it blue. It's blue, but it's not even or permanent, and it's noticeable that it's not actually a blue flower. The other tactic is to feed the flower blue dyed water from its roots and let it absorb the color. Every cell of the flower has blue water, and the petals have a clean and natural look that makes it impossible to notice that the flower was ever white. If you're the flower, then mindset is like dipping or spraying the flower. Identity is like the flower becoming a blue flower by absorbing the blue color into every cell of its being. I know which flower I want to be."

She blew my mind with that. She was also right. I would also want to make the change from the root.

"The great part is that success, for me and anyone who makes an identity shift, only happens by taking consistent and powerful actions. Big actions and stable, productive habits. So, the way you make a shift is, in fact, by doing the work to achieve goals while BECOMING the kind of person who achieves those goals. That way it becomes normal and even easy to achieve more in life on autopilot.

"I'm telling you, Ken, a shift at an identity level is the only way to make a permanent transformation in your life. In order to make an identity shift, you must upgrade how you operate to elevate your life and, if you let me, I'll show you exactly how.

"First, you'll have to let go of the ego, which is going to want to protect your pride and fight against the work you'll have to do.

It will trigger excuses so you don't lose pride when you're faced with areas of your life that you need to upgrade.

"Just like a couple hours ago, when you got mad at me for being mad at you for showing up late. We both know you were in the wrong, but your pride and ego reared up, without you even deeply thinking about it, and you tried to protect your ego from being attacked."

There she goes again with the zingers to my soul.

"An upgraded identity will combat that while making life easier and lighter as you succeed even more."

I took a death breath. Rocked back into my chair. Stared at two loving brown eyes that stared back at me. And let out a sigh before responding. "OK, Christine. First off, I want to apologize for being late, and you're right, I shouldn't have been late. Or, at least, I should have called you. That was disrespectful. To be honest, you've pegged me. I'm stuck, behind on my goals, and no matter how hard I push, it's like trying to move a stubborn elephant.

"I'm sold. I'm ready to do something about my situation. I want to elevate my life because if I'm being truthful, I'm burned out and breaking down more and more inside.

"How do I upgrade how I operate?"

"Ken, it's simple. You need to make an identity shift."

"OK. I'm ready, but first, you know I'm kind of a skeptic and need to know the ins and outs before I fully commit to something. So, I have to know—who's the guy that taught you all of this, how'd he figure this all out, and what exactly goes into making an identity shift?"

"Well, Ken, his name is Anthony Trucks, and you don't have to go too far to get those answers. He's actually been with us this entire time. He wrote the whole conversation we just had."

Wait what? Yes, I wrote that entire conversation.

It's like the movie *Never Ending Story*.

Well, what would you expect? I'm the author. Is this weird? I just broke the fourth wall and talked to you. Kind of like a Deadpool movie. Yes, I'm a Marvel fan. Well, I'm really just a fan of great stories and the effect they have on us as people. We learn and experience so much through story. That's why I'm going to spend the remainder of this book sharing impactful stories to solidify this identity shift concept in ways that will literally change the way you see yourself, the world, possibility, and what it takes to succeed.

Since we're going to spend time with interesting and valuable stories, I think it makes sense to start with the story that gave rise to this book. My personal story.

REFLECTION SECTION

Own Your Shift – Did anything in this story sound familiar? Do any of Ken's thoughts or behaviors remind you of yourself? If so, which ones?

This book is all about identity and it's going to teach you more about yourself and how to become more of who you desire to be. In order to clearly chart a path between where you are now and where you want to go we first need to figure out where you truly are right now.

Scan the QR code below or go to **www.SlowOrGo.co** to take the Slow Or Go Quiz to figure out what identity type you have now, how it's affecting you, and how you can shift it using The Shift Method and this book you're reading now.

SCAN ME

CHAPTER 1

IDENTITY & A.T.

I was once told that the true power of changing someone's life comes when the message shared flows from the messenger truly tasked with carrying it, and, after looking back at my life, I believe this message was one I was meant to share. It is my hope that the concepts presented in this book will peel back a curtain to a part of yourself you never knew existed, which will give you the opportunity to change your life like I did.

The journey of these words landing on the following pages, and my love-hate relationship with identity, started back in 1983.

With tears streaming down her pale white face, just missing the straggling wisps of her black hair, my mom leaned down to kiss my tiny three-year-old forehead right before she handed my right hand to a strange woman.

The woman's hand engulfed my tiny fingers as she gave me a quick tug and forcefully guided me towards a black Crown Victoria, doing her best to keep my tiny body from turning around to look at my mom with a worried, sad, and confused face.

Five minutes earlier, I was happily playing with toys in my tiny apartment living room by myself. I didn't have a worry in the world. I was a big brother, and I helped my mom with my three siblings all the time. My stepdad seemed like a nice guy, and he treated me well. I loved my mom, and I loved my life. Then my mom called me out to the back of our apartment. I saw her tears, and my life would never be the same again.

Before I knew it, I was buckled into the front seat. I turned around to see my three siblings all in the backseat crying. The car started up, and we drove away while I longingly looked at the crying face of my mom. I didn't know it at the time, but my mom had just given all of her kids away to a heinous foster care system that would all but destroy our childhoods. I went from home to home, being hit for no reason, put in chicken coops to chase chickens in the hopes of catching one to earn a meal for the night, repeatedly being pushed in a shopping cart down hills towards moving traffic, and forced to lick the bottoms of neighborhood kids' shoes until my tongue bled. After five foster homes in three years, I made it to my sixth and final home at six years old, but this wasn't your typical family.

I grew up poor and I was the only foster kid, and only black kid, in this all-white family of eight. My mom in this home, Gina Renea Hart, unconditionally loved me, and it was something I'd never experienced before. We didn't have much money growing up, but we did have dysfunction and love. During this time, I endured eight years of mental and emotional trauma from my biological mom while living with this family. She'd miss scheduled visits, make up lies for why she missed, and never allow me to play youth sports, even though all of my friends did. I especially hated Fridays, when all of my friends would wear their sports teams' jerseys to school.

Then, one day, at the age of 14, I was able to stand up in court in front of my real mom and tell her I no longer wanted her to be my mom anymore. This severed her parental rights and allowed me to be adopted by this family that grew to love me and that I had finally grown to love back. I was free, and for the first time that I could remember, I was 100 percent sure that the bed I woke up in that morning would be the one I would go to sleep in at night.

I wish it was all fairy tales from there, but let's be real—life doesn't work like that. Deep down I was ashamed to be the adopted black foster kid in an all-white family. I was entering high school, and we all know how crazy a time high school is, especially if you're still trying to figure out who you are in this crazy world. I had no defined identity and I seemed to always be searching for it. All parts of me seemed to be jammed in a tiny brain and heart that couldn't make any sense of things.

After adoption, I could finally play youth sports, even though I was four to six years behind some of my peers. So, I tried to find myself in football, but I sucked. On top of that, my adoptive mom got diagnosed with multiple sclerosis and my older brother shipped off to the military, leaving me alone. I was lost trying to find out who in the hell I was. Like you'd expect, I just threw my hands up and gave up. I felt like a lonely nobody loser and I assumed I was doomed to be left behind in life. So I "checked out" inside of my head and heart and assumed I was going to slide into the background of life and just get by somehow.

Statistically, I was headed to homelessness and/or prison. In any prison in America, 75 percent of the inmates are former foster kids. Over 51 percent of the homeless population has spent time in foster care, and 1 percent or less of us foster kids graduate from college. We just aren't set up to have success in life, unfortunately, and although I've beaten the odds now, I was NOT beating them at that moment in time.

Then something happened that quickly shifted my trajectory from prison to a promising future. It was a collection of 12 words from a 15-year-old girl that literally changed my entire life. I remember trying to take a nap, and struggling, with my head on the desk in the back right corner of Mr. Howell's English class in the lower-level, portable classroom. I had my black parka over my head, but I could, however, clearly hear the conversation between two girls sitting on the love seat to the right of me. One girl said to the other girl, having no idea anyone was listening, something that was an incredible gift to me at that moment.

"Well, the reason I'm so bad is because I'm in foster care."

"How was that a gift?" you might ask.

Well, when was the last time someone said, out loud, your excuse for choosing to give up or be mediocre? I'm going to guess it's possibly never. It was a gift because it snapped me out of my self-pity and made me realize just how stupid my excuse sounded as a reason to give up on having a great life. Hell, I was only 15 years old. I'd barely hit puberty and I assumed everything was over and I had no chance of anything getting better.

I went home that day and sat on the corner of my bed in confusion. My heart was sick at the thought that I might sound just like that girl if I was asked my excuse by someone. I stood up, looked myself in the eyes in the mirror on my wall, and I made a verbal declaration to myself...

"Anthony, you're going to be great. YOU are going to be great!"

ONE LIFE-CHANGING DECISION

At the time, I didn't know how great my potential actually was. I felt like being great was being able to get girls' phone numbers, taking care of my grades, and being better at sports. Little did I know, I was about to lay the foundation of what would come to be an unexpected life with multiple shifts of my identity that would take me on a rollercoaster of dark valleys and vibrantly bright mountain tops.

The next six months, between football seasons, I worked my ass off. I ran routes every day. Lifted weights when I was allowed into the weight room. Laid on my back and caught 500 balls a day because I never wanted to drop a football again. I transformed my skill sets. And I transformed my identity from a kid who thought he could be a great football player—even though none of his teammates did—to becoming that great football player and knowing in my bones I deserved success. My body, my identity, and eventually, my life changed forever.

That girl gave me a gift that day that changed my entire life, and I have come to learn that what happened in that window of time between my freshman and sophomore season is a lesson that we all need to learn. In this book, I'll be unpacking exactly what hidden lessons and teachable concepts, rooted in neuroscience and psychology, are tucked away inside of those moments because they're game changing when you embrace and apply them.

Please know that I'm not an actual research scientist that has been in a lab cooking up experiments. I'm a former NFL athlete who, after having a major identity crisis, has dedicated his life and work to understanding identity so I can help you make a shift like I have. I've spent thousands of hours obsessively studying and mastering this concept of identity to make life easier for you than it was for me. So, forgive me if my lingo isn't scientific and if I sound like a regular guy because I am. I'm a regular guy with an unexplainable, irregular desire and calling to help you reach your full potential.

See, I went from being one of the suckiest players on the team to an all-star who got moved up to varsity as a sophomore and even earned a football scholarship to the University of Oregon two years later. I started operating at a higher level, and it paid off beyond my wildest dreams. At my core, my identity, I was a different level human. I was blessed to become a starter at Oregon my true sophomore year. In fact, my first collegiate start took place on national television. We won the game, I earned a game ball, and I got to meet my biological dad for the first time because, months earlier, I had just found out who he was, and he agreed to drive five hours to meet me in Mississippi. I was able to get closure on a key piece of my identity—where I had come from. It was powerful for me because I had recently become a father just nine months earlier, with my high school sweetheart, as a sophomore in college, eight hours from any family support system.

College seemed to fly by with my fiancée and I both juggling college classes, a baby, a new dad in my life, and me playing D1 football. It was difficult, but, man, was it fun. Talk about an identity-shifting year.

I'd always wanted to be a dad because of my situation growing up, and I wanted to do better than was done for me. I had a fiancée whom I loved deeply because, I think, having issues with my mom growing up, I developed a strong connection with any woman in my life. This girl was my HEART. Words cannot describe the love I had for her as the mother of my child and how deeply I'd come to love her and all things about her. Actually, a year before we had gotten pregnant, I had already proposed to her at 18 years old because I knew she was the one for me.

After four years battling injury, life, and relationship hardships in college, I got the opportunity to play football in the NFL—the highest level in the WORLD for my sport. Life just seemed to be getting better and better. Not only had I beaten the previous odds, but now I had ascended into a world where less than half of a percent of football players get a chance to play. Now don't get me wrong; I had my battles in the NFL—preparing for the draft and fighting to get signed, fighting for a job once signed, getting cut, and the process recycling twice before landing with the Pittsburgh Steelers in 2007.

I had finally made it to a team and had earned a level of acceptance within the team where I felt like a true fit. At the two other teams, the Redskins and Buccaneers, before the Steelers, I was just a low-level guy that nobody seemed to care about. I went to practice every single day feeling like an outcast and wondering if I would even have a job come tomorrow. I had imposter syndrome flowing through my identity the whole time I was in the NFL because I questioned if I even belonged.

In the NFL you learn to live and operate daily at an incredibly high level with a heavy heart full of anxiety. With the Steelers I had FINALLY climbed the ranks to become one of the "guys" on special teams. In case that doesn't mean much to you, this means you're probably going to make the team and finally feel like you've been accepted and have peace in your heart...and some money in your bank account.

I was on cloud nine, and life was amazing. I was recently married, had a son, had graduated college with my degree two days before training camp, and life was finally feeling GREAT! The first pre-season game had arrived. I remember walking out of that tunnel donning a Pittsburgh Steelers uniform on August 8, 2008 and the chills that ran through my body. At one point in the game, I headed out onto the field as a linebacker. We were playing the Philadelphia Eagles, and I watched their offense line up for a play as I got into position.

The QB gets under center to snap the ball and... "HIKE!"

Little did I know, this was the moment my world would begin to come crashing down.

The ball was snapped. I ran left to make the tackle. I tripped over my teammate and fell to the ground. As I'm getting up, the offensive lineman meant to block me jumps in the air and lands my back and...BAM! My shoulder is torn. Now, at that time, with adrenaline flowing mid game, I didn't even notice it, and I didn't until the next morning, but when I did notice it, I could tell it was serious. I would soon learn that I needed surgery and this was the end of my season. My previous teammates would go on to win a Super Bowl while I watched at home on the couch after surgery.

I was at home, coming to terms with the fact that I wasn't on a team, dealing with rehabbing my shoulder and needing to find something to do with my time while I waited to try and get picked up again by another team. Before I knew it, I was getting an itch to be productive. So I opened a gym in my hometown to make a living and also give back. My gym was called Trucks Training, and after getting my degree in kinesiology, and being the first in my family to graduate college, I decided it was time to put that education to use.

At that same time, in 2009, my wife and I had just found out we were having twins.... TWINS!! Hooooly crap, is that scary. What was worse is that running a gym was HARD, and I wasn't making any money back, even though I was there from 6:00 a.m. to 10:00 p.m., trying to make ends meet after I'd invested a lot of money into opening this gym. If I'm being honest, though, I was also dealing with the identity crisis stirring inside of me for not being the NFL guy at the moment.

Then, there I was, one day in 2009, sitting in at the front desk of my gym, when a Harley comes rumbling up and parks four feet outside my door. A hardened-looking guy in a black leather vest gets off the bike, gets something out of his side bag, then turns to walk in my door. He walks in with a stoic look on his face and just scans the room before turning to me on his right side. He saunters up to the counter and looks me in my eyes.

"Are you Anthony Trucks?"

"Ya"

"Here you go."

I didn't know what to expect when I grabbed the envelope, but when I opened it, I saw a letter from my landlord, whom I hadn't been able to pay for three months. I had two weeks to pay four times the money I had in my bank account at that moment, or I would be evicted and sued, which would bankrupt me.

I fought for the next two weeks to find a way to just avoid going bankrupt and losing all the money I had just put into this gym. My wife was pissed and had lost faith in me as a man and father of our three kids. I was still at the gym from 6:00 a.m. to 10:00 p.m. every day and neglecting her and my family, trying to make something of my name. What was worse is when I looked in the mirror, I could slowly see my NFL body turning into a dad bod from the eating, stress, and lack of exercise, even though I still had dreams of going back and playing.

Not soon after this eviction was looming, I was sitting in my office one early morning and got a call from my NFL agent who asked me to sit down because we had a hard conversation ahead of us. I hadn't yet retired, and I still had these hopes that I could go back and play in the NFL soon.

"Anthony, you got an offer from the Bills, but they want to put a waiver on your shoulder, which means if you hurt your shoulder, no one is going to cover it. You may never be able to fully function, and it could be very bad for your family and your ability to provide for them in the long run. You have to choose to either take this contract, which will be similar to every offer you are going to get and which I wouldn't recommend, or you make the hard choice of hanging up your jersey."

Inside it felt like an eternity passed before I parted my lips for the first words to escape my lips.

"Well, Drew..." Tears started running down my face. "I'm going to have to hang up my jersey."

After the call ended, I sat there for another hour, ugly crying like a big bear because I received a wave of emotion in realizing my entire identity of the football player had just been ripped away from me. I had lost the thing that made me...*me*.... I unknowingly floated into despair.

I hadn't realized it all my life, but I'd been navigating countless shifts in my identity to get here, and now everything was tumbling down in my life. I'd lost my football identity, my healthy strong body, my self-confidence in a career to provide for my family, and I'd soon come to find that I would lose my family and my marriage. Like so many others, I stumbled into a catastrophic identity crisis.

MY WORLD CAME TUMBLING DOWN

There we were, in front of P.F. Chang's in Hawaii. My wife was on her phone and barely paying attention to me. This had been going on all day, and I couldn't figure out what exactly was going on. So, I slowly snuck up behind her, and I saw that she was texting another guy. In fact, she was texting the same guy I'd already suspected she was too close to and had already asked her to stop talking to. She'd downloaded a secret app on her phone to hide her actions.

I snatched her phone before she noticed I was standing there and took off down the street so she couldn't stop me from reading what she was texting. Let's just say that what I read shattered me to the depths of whatever soul, security, and self-confidence I had left as a man. I now knew things I couldn't wrap my head around and I hated her for what she'd done, but my love for her was so deep I didn't know what to do.

The rest of the trip was obviously ruined, and I was now met with the realization that I had not only lost my identity as an athlete, a confident man who could provide, but I was now looking at the likely removal of my family and marriage from my identity as well. I fell into a fog of despair that slowly but surely was bringing me to my rock bottom.

After vacation, and the longest return home in my life, I had to go back to my business, where I was expected to be this happy person for others and dig deeeeeep to find and give joy that I didn't have. Every ounce of my body wanted to curl into a ball in the corner and cry my eyes out. I kept asking myself, *How did I go from the incredibly happy human and NFL player, on top of the world, to this?*

Every day and night was filled with insecurity and fights, and my wife, at one point, made it clear to me as I walked out the door that I was not the man she wanted to call her husband anymore. Internally, I was broken. That night, I ended up going to my buddy Derek's house to watch the UFC fights, and I remember sitting on the couch and not making a sound for three hours. If you know me, then you know this is beyond out of character for me. My best friend Jason took notice, and when I went to leave, Jason walked out with me and stopped me right before I was getting into my car.

Jason was my post to lean on during the tough times and he knew how hard I was fighting to keep my marriage and not accept what was really going on inside. I was always justifying, and he was always trying to clear my mind. As he walked with me to the car, he stopped me and said five words that punched a hole in my heart.

"Ant, this is your reality..."

Writing this right now brings back a rush of emotions that feel so familiar and foreign at the same time. Those words cut me to my core and unleashed something that had been pent up inside for months since the Hawaii vacation and all the hardships that ensued afterwards.

I got in the car and I felt a rush of pain so intense I can genuinely not even describe it. Imagine not being able to breathe, stop tears from pouring down your face, or stop the pain that is so heavy you can actually *feel* it deep to your core. I couldn't stop it, and ALL I wanted was for it to stop. In my emotional state and not thinking clearly, I decided that it was time to end the pain the only way I knew how. To end my life.

I had lost everything that made me me at this point. I was smack dab in the middle of an identity crisis unlike anything I'd ever experienced, and if THIS is what my life was going to be, I wanted zero part of it anymore. I texted my friends, family, my wife, and Jason too, "Please tell my children who their father was," and I drove off as fast as I could.

It was 10:00 p.m., and I had no clue exactly where I was going but I knew I was in search of something to end it. I got on the freeway and headed down Highway 4 east. At a certain point, I was on Balfour Road, on the way to Stockton, and I decided the simplest way to go was to get some rat poison, eat it, and lay down in the back seat of my car. Thankfully, it was too late, and no stores were open. So, I parked next to a gas station in Stockton California and just cried and cried. After about an hour or so, the wave of pain had started to subside, and I started coming to terms with the reality I was facing if I stayed in this world. It wasn't going to be easy.

Police showed up. Apparently, they'd tracked my GPS. I was able to convince them I was just fine, and they sent me home. I showed up to find more than 30 people in front of my house, all looking for me. The shame was overwhelming, as you can imagine. I tucked my head and faced the music. All of these people who'd come to care for and love me were hurt by me, and it made it feel even worse. I just wanted to run away from it all again, but I had to face it.

Two days later, I was somehow back at work, trying to act like nothing had happened, and one of my buddies, who was a trainer at my gym, a friend, and someone who I'd played HS football with, pulled me into the back office to have a talk. Richie was not the kind of guy you expect to share his emotions. Typical alpha guy's guy and one hell of a friend. His words were simple yet profoundly powerful in planting a seed that has led me to this exact stage in my life.

"Ant, when I found out what was going on, I threw up, man..."

"I'm sorry, Richie. Seriously."

"You need to know why though... I thought I'd lost a hero."

"A hero?"

"You don't realize it, but everyone knows what you've gone through in life and what you have accomplished. We're all inspired by you and your life. You mean more to so many than you even know, man."

I was legitimately confused by this because I'd never considered the fact that my life was one that was inspiring to others. I'd always been ashamed of my life and angry because it made no sense for all of this craziness to always seem to happen to me. I felt like I kind of just tried to put my head down and work because I knew what my life could be like if I didn't. Not to mention, I always wanted to do right by my adoptive mom, who'd given me so much love over the years to keep me from being a statistic. I'd always lived for me and didn't really think about what it could mean to live for others.

This conversation was one that planted a seed that made me realize that maybe, just maybe, there could be a reason for the horrible experiences in my life and something greater could come out of it all. Maybe there was a larger potential and purpose for my life than hanging on to the past and assuming that nothing could ever top the NFL. I actually started thinking to myself, *What if instead of inspiring people by accident, I did it on purpose?*

It was a seed that was planted but one I didn't have any intentions of watering for a while....

THE FOG & MOVING FORWARD

I went on with my life as a shell of my former self because I didn't know what to do with everything. My business was on thin ice, week after week, for the next three years, and I blamed it on the economy and the community. I bought tons of programs, books, and joined coaching groups for my business as tools and strategies to grow my income, and nothing ever seemed to work. I was spinning my wheels, and business didn't seem to be for me. On top of the issues with being away from home, I couldn't even help with bills. Every two weeks I was distraught with anxiety, wondering how I would be able to cover payroll and then rent AND payroll. I was treading water financially and it felt like every week I was gasping for air, on the verge of drowning.

I ended up getting a divorce, and in my mind, it was all my ex-wife's fault. Then I got into another relationship a year later that failed and blamed it all on the girl and her needing to work on herself. I never played with my kids or put their sports as a priority and blamed it on the gym that needed me to be there consistently. I hated myself inside, and it was showing up in my life and how I operated, even though I tried to bury it and show everyone on the outside that I was fine.

I took no blame and, therefore, never worked on Anthony. Then, one day, I woke up next to a woman I barely knew, and a rush of shame fell over me. Who I'd become disgusted me. I would hate it if my kids saw me or if my kids grew up to do what I was doing. I'd fallen from my faith and was steadily sliding downhill.

Then, God woke me up one day by taking something big from my life and giving me something heavy to carry all in the same moment. April 15, 2014, I was sitting in a hospital room, at the right side of my mom's hospital bed, holding her right hand, looking up at a beeping heart rate monitor, with my dad and grandma on my mom's left side. We watched my mom inhale...and exhale her final breath. In one instant, God took my mom from me.

Then, through my tears, He gave me a heavy cross to bear. My mom unconditionally loved me, and that love created the man writing this book, who is consistently reaching to achieve his full potential because of the fact that MS took my mom's dreams and ability to reach her full potential in life. God decided it was time to water that seed Richie had planted in me three years before. He gave me the task of giving that same unconditional love to the world, to YOU, to help others reach their full potentials as a way to carry on and honor her memory. I realized it was time to wake up and make a decision to be GREAT again.

I started by taking ownership for my life and all the things that happened. I realized and owned my role in my marriage failing. My role in my other relationship failing. My role in my business struggling. My role in my kids not having a great father. God also provided me the means and a method to bring this vision to life. He gave me a contract that provided an opportunity to shift careers and a mentor with a method for turning my mess into a message to become a beacon of hope for the world.

I dug in. Through the ridiculous emotional and financial pain that came with the actions I was deathly afraid of taking, I started the process of changing my life, and changing those around me, on purpose, for once. Without knowing it at the time, I shifted my actions, thoughts, beliefs, mindset, habits, and ego. It was long and hard work that took over four years to successfully accomplish.

Those shifts allowed me to finally get back to being that joyous and confident man I'd lost sight of so many years before. Not only that, but I kept on moving ahead faster and farther than I'd ever thought possible. I realized there WAS something greater than the NFL for my life and I began to seek and reach the next levels of my potential in pursuit of my highest level. I have come to find that this is a superpower of mine that I can actually TEACH. You can only give something that you have, and through my crazy journey, this is something I have and want to give to the world because of what this skillset (superpower) has done for my life.

I went from being a guy that no one knew to being in a private mastermind group with Brendon Burchard and over 30 world-changing humans, flying in private jets, speaking in front of thousands at a time, being on multiple television shows, consulting for Amazon, Lockheed Martin, and PayPal, and even speaking for T-Mobile's entire company. Believe me, I look in the mirror at times, wondering how in the hell I ended up in this place, but I know it's because I learned how to master an identity shift—something you're about to master as you read and apply what you're about to learn in this book.

My businesses have now brought in over seven figures because I operate at a ridiculously high rate from an identity level. It's WHO I AM to execute. Any tools or strategies I invest in are applied, and they actually work, or I find a way to make them work. I'm in great shape and take care of my body with joy and ease. My kids have a happy and present father who spends solo time with each of them every week. Best of all, after three years divorced, I remarried my ex-wife and have the most incredible marriage I could ever imagine. I'd seriously put my marriage strength against any other in the world. My heart is so full right now, and I just want to help everyone I can experience this level of fulfillment I can. That means you.

There is one thing I am incredibly good at that I found out I was forced to start mastering as far back as three years old without knowing it. Something that inherently became a superpower of mine throughout life that made itself known to me just a few years ago. Something I'd utilized by sheer survival and, had I known earlier that I could intentionally do it, it would have saved me years of stress, struggle, time, and money on the path to operating at my highest level to reach my full potential.

It's an identity shift, and I'm going to give you a gift that I never received but wish I had. I'm going to shortcut the path to shifting your identity by unpacking the science and psychology behind this process and sharing my stories as well as others', which will provide you with a powerful transformational process for your life accompanied by reflection questions and exercises you can use to explore what you learn in real time to anchor the concepts and make immediate shifts in your own life.

You'll come to realize that I love sharing concepts in metaphors, and there's one that I want to leave you with before you head deeper into these pages.

THE KEY TO A GREAT LIFE

As much as I love my wife, I don't love the fact that she misplaces something almost weekly. Usually it's her keys, but at times, it's her phone, purse, etc. Think back to a time when you were walking around your house frantically looking for your car keys because you knew that the only way you were going to leave that place to get where you needed to be was by having that single item to access all of the vehicle's available features.

You're running around the house, tossing pillows, digging in drawers, lifting furniture, checking old pants, and about to freak out because you're getting later and later by the minute. You can't for the life of you figure out how you're ever going to leave. You finally just about give up and sit on your wooden kitchen chair, then hear a crunch come from your butt. You tilt to the side to find that your keys were in your back pocket this entire time, and you now have the ability to access everything available to you to reach your desired destination. What you needed was always with you and you just didn't notice it.

Your identity is much like your car keys in this metaphor. It's the key to access everything you need to succeed, and although you've been running around your whole life, trying to find the key to success, it's always been right there with and within you. You just haven't found the key until now, and once you put it into the ignition, you'll be able to access everything that's available to you to reach your desired destination. It's time to start turning pages, just like you'd turn the key in the ignition, to get you where you're meant to be in this life.

REFLECTION SECTION

Shift Sucks Sometimes – Can you recall a time in your life when you felt the way I did during my personal low points?

What does that shift mean? – I gave my life a positive meaning to strive for greatness. Where in your life can you give a positive meaning to a difficult situation?

Real Shift – This is real life. As we proceed, I want you to be present with the reality you're experiencing and be able to really feel it, even if you've avoided looking at things in the past. What's one thing that comes to mind that you should address?

CHAPTER 2

COMP-YOU-TER?

It was 1935, and there was a chill in the air on another winter night in Germany. In an unassuming house, there was a man hard at work in his parents' living room. He was working tirelessly on an invention that would come to revolutionize the world as humanity knows it. His name was Konrad Zuse, and he is credited as the inventor of the first programmable computer called the Turing-Complete Z3, which, after years of work, was patented in 1941. Without Zuse, I quite literally wouldn't be writing this book. I'm sure at some point, someone would have invented the computer, but no one knows exactly how much longer the world would have had to wait.

Since then, the evolution of the computer and the increase in technological speed has been exponential. In fact, in 1965, the CEO of Fairchild Semiconductor, Gordon Moore, made a fascinating claim. He noticed that the speed and power of computers double every 18 months without an increase in size or consumption of power. At the time, he presumed it would hold for another decade, but in 1975, he adjusted his claims and found that it was still doubling every 24 months. This has held true since 1975 and, even without any empirical data, has been widely accepted as a law. Moore's Law.

I wonder if Konrad Zuse ever could have imagined what the computer has become. The power his invention had has increased so vastly that it has changed the world and, in fact, changed the biology of the people in this world. We get arthritis and rounded backs from our interactions with computers and digital devices. It is so deeply woven into the fabric of our lives that we can't even imagine a world without the computer.

PREPARE FOR PROGRESS

Now I bet you're wondering why in the world I'm giving you some random history lesson on the invention of the computer, processing speed and power, or anything to do with the rate of its improvement. Well, it's because the realization I made completely changed my life.

At this very moment, I'm sitting at my kitchen table in Walnut Creek, California at 9:03 a.m. on December 6, 2020. One of the craziest years our world has experienced since the 2008 recession. It genuinely feels like we're all in a movie with a bad script. I'm writing this very book on my MacBook Pro. I had to get it upgraded to handle the increased bandwidth needed for the additional computer equipment I've purchased for the purpose of online meetings since I'm working from home now like everyone else.

I've had to download and/or learn more new programs on my computer than ever before in order to function with the outside world. Prezi Video, Zencaster, Streamyard, Microsoft Teams, Webex, GoToMeeting, Zoom, Garageband, Airtable, Shift, Adobe, Yellow Duck, and the list could go on and on. All these programs have literally allowed my life to run smoother and be more enjoyable because they all bring something special to the table functionality wise. Most days I find myself looking at a menu bar packed full of different colored icons representing each program.

My MacBook computer is simultaneously running all of these programs in the background and keeping them functioning so they can be used whenever I need them, without me having to think about it. Then, when I start using them, other hardware becomes necessary—the screen, keyboard, graphics card, audio card, USB plugs, and so forth. The processing power of my computer, the RAM (random access memory), and the other hardware on my computer allows for this to happen, and although it's literally always running, even when my computer is asleep, I don't even notice the computer processing or using other hardware. Without the computer's processor and accompanying hardware, the programs would literally be useless.

Then you have another integral aspect of your computer. I'd argue it's the most critical part. On my MacBook I have OS/X. On PCs, you'll find Windows. On ThinkPads, you may find Linux. These are all what we call operating systems. Like Konrad Zuse's very early invention, it's a programmable system. While the physical processing power and other hardware peripherals may depict the physical capabilities of the computer, the operating system is the link between the physical capabilities of the computer and the actual interaction with the programs that make my life easier and more enjoyable. When you want to add a program to your arsenal of helpful tools, you have to make sure it's compatible with your operating system, or it won't work at all. It's a symphony of connections, and they all come together to make it possible for me to write this book for you right now.

So, look at it like this. I'm using Google Chrome to use Google Docs to write these words right now, and I'm listening to music through my headphones. In order for this to happen, I had to have a computer that has the hardware necessary to bring the processor to life along with the other hardware devices. I then had to have an operating system that could function with all the other programs I have installed on my computer and still be able to run my music and the Google Chrome browser app. This seamless functionality makes it seem almost effortless to do such a complicated task. Just think of how many years of research, development, testing, failing, and so much more went into the ability for me to listen to a song and write a book on an electronic screen in 2020.

SYSTEM UPGRADE

Something interesting happened in April of this year. I had a desire to adjust my life, due to unforeseen COVID-19 circumstances, and start running my entire business from home on my 13" MacBook Pro. The limited screen space was a problem. I needed to make some upgrades. I got two more 27" monitors for my office so I could have more computer workspace than my tiny 13" screen. I added a better camera so the visuals people had when meeting with me would look more professional because I wanted to start doing virtual presentations. I upgraded my audio system by adding a new microphone and audio device to run the microphone. All of these upgrades, and a few more, came with the need for more programs to be downloaded so they could be used by my computer. Not to mention the increased pull on the operating system and the current programs I was already using.

I started getting these constant pop-ups sliding in from the top right of my screen, asking me to upgrade programs in the middle of my meetings or when I was deep in a time block and trying to complete a task I was working on. So, I obviously snoozed the alerts because I didn't have the time or desire to wait for the computer to download the information it needed and then take even more time to upload it all. So, I continued on with my work, snoozing for 24 hours again and again while still continuing to use the programs. I was frustrated and didn't like the thought of having to wait for the system to download the updates and then have to wait longer to let them upload and install on my computer. I didn't want to take that time and I didn't care because I didn't see the importance of it. "Ain't nobody got time for that!"

At the same time, I kept getting hiccups in the system when I was using the programs. The computer kept getting overheated, and I didn't know why. Then I noticed programs were running super slowly. It took forever for them to start up, and when they did, it seemed like they were moving slower than a snail. I tried turning off every program I wasn't using that was accessing the internet in hopes that it could fix the issue, but it persisted. No matter what I randomly tried, nothing seemed to improve the situation.

My meetings kept dropping, music kept pausing, files took forever to download, some files wouldn't open at all, programs got stuck with the spinning wheel of death, and even my battery seemed to die faster than ever before. One time, I even decided to start the computer in safe mode in the hopes that it could work that way for my needs, but it cut off certain functions of my computer, and that made it even harder to do what I wanted and needed to do. So I googled the problem and came to find that the issue was something I hadn't even considered.

My computer's processor and RAM were being taxed. My computer's processor and other hardware were being overloaded by what they were now being asked to do, which made it more difficult to give the operating system the power it needed to operate. This led to the computer overheating, which slowed everything down and even shut off the computer at times. As much as I was trying to get what I wanted done with this computer, as is, I was going to continue to run into the same issues. I could either chance the computer burning up and ruining it, accept going slow the entire time, or be OK with not being able to experience what I was trying to experience with the new hardware upgrades I had made because the programs just wouldn't work. Not to mention that I kept getting all these alerts to update my programs.

I just wanted everything to work. I wanted my programs to run smoothly without crashing, slowing, or giving me that spinning wheel of death. I just want to be able to use and enjoy the hardware, programs, and files I invested in. When I reached my wits' end, I called someone who I trust with computers and told them exactly what I was experiencing. What he told me led to a profound realization. He broke everything down to me in a way that made my issues crystal clear.

He told me that if my goal was to get the programs and files to run smoothly, I needed to start from the bottom up and take a look at everything involved. My computer itself didn't have the hardware it needed internally to succeed, and, in fact, that's why everything was failing. The processor wasn't strong enough or fast enough to support the new additions, so it would run itself hard, get hot, and shut down—something that could actually damage the computer permanently.

The hardware, while great, was slowing everything down and adding too much work to the processor. The programs I was trying to run weren't working because not only was the processor being taxed, but the operating system itself needed an upgrade to be able to handle everything. On top of that, all the updates I kept snoozing should have been installed because they actually help with bugs and function fixes that make it easier for the computer to do its job. So, in a weird way, I was actually snoozing my success without knowing it.

I asked him what exactly I needed to do so I could get what I wanted. He was, again, clear about one thing: if I expected to have these new hardware pieces plugged in, like the screens and new microphone, and have the success I wanted, then the computer would need a better processor. That way I would have the ability to give the computer's operating system the power it needed to operate the programs with ease.

Then, I would need to make sure I was consistently keeping up with the updates so the programs would work perfectly at all times and never give the operating system or processor any issues. This would mean I could get the most out of every program, and actually multiple programs at once, without ever overheating the system. As an added bonus, he recommended I get a laptop cooler as well so the temperature would stay down and help the processor run even smoother for longer without ever getting any damage.

So I did just that. In upgrading everything, I went with a computer that had the same physical aspects (screen, keyboard, touchpad, etc.) but double the processing speed and RAM. It also had an upgraded operating system, which made it incredibly easy to run all the programs I wanted to run along with making it possible to operate with the new screens, mic, etc., without overheating or shutting down the computer. I can now fully experience the vision I had of what it would look and feel like with everything running properly. Other people got to see and engage with me in a powerful way, and I even got a red glowing laptop cooling base so it had the perfect environment to function at its peak. Upgrading the operations of the computer has allowed me to elevate every aspect involved with it.

LIFE UPGRADE

So what does this have to do with you at all?

EVERYTHING.

In my personal opinion, this is, in fact, the most important concept of this book, and I'm going to cut right to the chase here. You are a biological computer, and everything you just read ties directly to you and your life. When I first settled into this thought during my weekly 60-minute thinking time, I got chills while sitting in my hammock.

Your physical body is the biological hardware of your computer in the same way the screen, keyboard, mouse, speakers, and every other physical piece of the computer is the "body" of the computer. Your feet, legs, torso, arms, hands, arms, and other parts are your actual body. Without the body, nothing else can be installed to make it run. It would quite literally be useless junk that would take up space. However, there is more to this biological computer of yours.

Inside of your physical body you have a tool that has named itself. Your brain. If your physical body is the body of your computer, then your physical brain is the processor of this biological computer of yours. Your brain is a processor, and it has chemical and electrical components that allow it to operate. When you try to add more to its functions, it can "overheat," just like an actual computer. Think of this like adding a new screen, microphone, etc., to a computer. Think about trying to figure out the way your new electronics work, buying some new material objects like a bow and arrow, buying your first house, and having to learn the ins and outs of everything, dealing with troublesome relationships, getting a new job, and so many other things you add or want to add to your life.

People fail to realize that there is a threshold you can cross into where your inputs are "too much" for your brain to handle. In a computer, the hardware runs hot and can run the risk of overheating and completely shutting down the computer and causing permanent damage. In your real life, you can get burned out, frustrated, overwhelmed, have a panic attack, a psychotic break, PTSD, and even get to the point of having a full system shutdown where you can cause permanent damage to your life by ending it, all because the processor of your brain isn't able to physically handle the load. It hasn't been upgraded to handle the things you have running all at once.

Far too many people wonder why they're unable to add all the things to their life that they desire—like new relationships, a new car, new house, more money, more impact, more influence, and essentially anything you would personally say after the word "more." They have zero clue that the root of the issue lies in how much their brain can actually process and handle at any given time at a physical level. This is something that can be improved over time through brain work, which can increase the bandwidth a human brain can handle. The science of neuroplasticity tells us that this is, in fact, possible and is the reason why some people are able to handle so much more than others and why those same people have so much more in life. This is why some people have what many would call success. They've been able to increase their mental capacity through active engagement of their brains.

Consider it this way. There are people easily lifting and warming up with weights in the gym that you may not be able to even pick up off the floor. How? Were they born like Hercules and inherited Godlike strength? Of course not. They started in the same place and over years of putting in effort they built up their strength and, in fact, make what's hard to you look easy.

The same applies to your mind. There are people who can handle long conversations, multiple meetings, kids, a spouse, giving presentations, working lunches, and countless emails, without so much as a stumble in productivity. They do it day in and day out, and it legitimately makes you think they must be on something. Truth is lifting that "weight" of a day is just a strength they developed along the way. So where you may shut down halfway through the day and need two days to recover, they just stack day after day with the same intensity while actually enjoying it. No wonder they're more successful. They can efficiently, and with high quality, output far more than your brain can consistently without burning out.

So it's not an accident; they aren't special. They've simply been able to increase their processing capabilities, through conscious actions, to handle more. By handling more I mean they can handle more stress and added load to their days, more consistently, and still go on with their lives with ease and the ability to actually take on more if they wanted to. They have increased bandwidth and capacity. They run things smoothly and make it look easy just like my upgraded MacBook has been able to do with all the new equipment and programs.

These "things" they're running smoothly to be able to experience great lives are what you'd call "programs" in a computer. Or apps on a mobile device. When I think about the Chrome program that allows me to browse the internet, I feel at ease. I know that if I run the program, it's going to work smoothly and efficiently while I'm on it. I know how fast I can download or stream movies and music. I know it will quickly work when I need it. When I think about opening a file on my computer to watch a movie, play music, or edit a presentation, I know there is a program that will make it possible to access that file's information and use it. This is what programs and files do for our computers. They make the computer useful and enjoyable.

In our lives, these programs and files carry different names. Programs are our relationships, careers, health, businesses, hobbies, projects, and so much more. Programs are the purpose of the computer, just as your flesh computer is worthless without everything it can do. The files in a computer are brought to life by our programs. In life, your files are information in the form of books, online courses and trainings, insights learned from others, experiences you have from life, and essentially anything that you take in as information that can help you. Your programs then bring those files to life and make them accessible. Like deep discussions with loved ones about something you learned. Applying the newest training you took to your profession. Or the wisdom gained from your mentor on how to scale your business. In the same way QuickTime or RealPlayer can bring a movie file to life so it can be watched, a book on relationships can only be brought to life in the "program" of your relationship.

Unfortunately, just like a computer system with poor processing power, your brain at its current abilities can only handle so much of the different programs you're trying to run simultaneously, such as your career, your health, learning new information, your relationships, your hobbies, etc., before shutting down. If you try to take on more, it usually stresses the system. That's why we're always trying to find balance because we're overloading our physical capabilities by overdoing it in one area or another. Then, on top of that, the programs start giving up alerts that they need updates. In your life, these updates come in the form of feedback, constructive criticism, or straight-up criticism that holds truths your ego doesn't want to accept in the moment.

Just like in a physical computer, we snooze everything because we don't care to "update" ourselves and we're too busy to take that time. So, as the updates come in for the programs, we snooze them. Your boss tells you that you need to do better work, and you ignore—snooze—it. Your clients tell you they want something more, but you ignore them, explain things away, or push things off because you don't want to deal with it. Your kids tell you they want to spend more time with you, but you make excuses so you don't have to take that time away. Your partner expresses discontent in your relationship, and you deflect the blame or ignore the issue completely.

These are just a few of the countless ways the programs in your life are telling you that they need an upgrade. Unfortunately, you snooze and ignore them completely, so they all run slow and put a strain on your processing power. You start having programs that are running so incredibly slowly that they're making zero progress and bogging you down. Kind of like starting a health journey that seems to stall and plateau. Other programs get stuck with the spinning wheel of death, much like a relationship that gets stuck in never-ending fights and arguing. Other programs simply crash mid use without saving, and you're stuck and frustrated, having to completely start over, just like a failed business or lost job. Without the updates, your programs will eventually run your processor (brain) at max until it burns out or they crash (overwhelm).

In life, many people, unfortunately, get to these burnout moments, and they do the equivalent of running your computer in safe mode. They start turning off the core programs and try to operate as simply as possible. They cut people off in their lives and try to do everything by themselves with no other programs, people, or support involved. This almost always fails because they don't have the full functionality of the system and, therefore, they'll never fully achieve the results they desire. Finally, they end up either crashing the computer, which no one wants, or making the decision to do what they've been avoiding. People are always in motion, and the thought of simply stopping drives people crazy. We're all simply too busy being busy, and we actually get so addicted to the pace, but an upgrade is a necessity whether it's a computer or our lives.

This leads us to the most critical aspect of this flesh computer of yours. The operating system. Your identity. In a computer, the operating system is such a crucial part because it helps determine and set the necessary pace of the processor, as well as determines if/when/how the updates of programs will take place. Your identity will determine whether you can or can't handle everything going on in your life. Unfortunately, like a computer, no one ever really thinks about the operating system, or their identity, and the thought of updating it feels a lot trickier. But it's literally the invisible key to making everything work.

When the computer is operating problematically, we seem to always first look at the hardware, the files, and then the programs, but never the operating system. This means people first look to improve their bodies, upgrade their car or house, start a business, or even take trips. If that doesn't work, they start looking at the files they have downloaded to see if they're the right files or if they have any viruses. They look at all the information they have and start blaming their issues on the wrong "files" or strategies and tactics being utilized. Finally, if that doesn't work, they start looking at the programs as the issue. So they start cutting off relationships, quitting their jobs, joining new groups, taking on new hobbies, or focusing on simply fixing the program. All of which end with no better results because they can't figure out why things are still running slowly and they're struggling to get the functionality they desire.

Sometimes we'll turn things off and on to reset the programs or the whole computer to hopefully fix the issues. Regardless of what we do, the operating software is rarely ever considered to be the issue. When you dig in, you actually find that the operating system, on top of determining the processing drain, also determines the types of programs that are even able to be loaded onto the computer. There are programs that run on a Mac that would never run on a PC. They can't even be installed. There are some programs have been designed for different operating systems, like Microsoft Word or Google Chrome, which have versions for different operating systems; however, I've found programs that seem great but don't work on my Mac. Some programs don't even have a Mac version, so I have to find a different program.

If you have a program you want to run, the only possible way to do it is by having a compatible operating system (identity). This means some "programs" in life simply won't work for you if they're not compatible with your identity, and that's just how it goes. You might want to have a certain career or start a business, but you find it's just not compatible with your identity. Maybe you love the idea of being an entrepreneur but you lack the ability or desire to take risks with your career. Or you're unable to identify with being heterosexual or monogamous in relationships. Even though you're trying to install those programs, they may not be a fit for your operating system (identity). Just because you want something to be part of your life does not mean that you can, or even should, have it installed on your operating system (identity). Your identity is not compatible with every program in the world, and that's OK. Seek and find a program that fits, and you may actually find a better program that doesn't overload your processor by taxing the operating system.

In addition to having up-to-date hardware (body) and programs, you need an up-to-date operating system (identity). In fact, when you try to install or update newer programs, even if they're compatible and the hardware is functional, you'll find it's impossible if the operating system hasn't been upgraded in a computer. If you don't have the right up-to-date OS/X version, you'll be unable to update to the current version of QuickTime.

So, picture yourself trying to update and elevate a relationship in your life, but your identity is so old school with its beliefs and ego that you can't, or won't, do what needs to be done to fix it. You want the "program" of your relationship to run better, but the update it needs is for you to communicate better or agree to different things in the bedroom. You don't believe in doing those things because "men don't do that" or "women shouldn't do that."

This is where an upgrade to the operating system is necessary. If you are able to upgrade the six core drivers of your identity, which you'll learn about in the next chapter, you'd be able to do what needs to be done in that relationship to not only fix it but make it thrive. It's an upgrade that's necessary to elevate your relationship.

Consider applying this concept of upgrading your identity to elevate your professional life. You want to launch and scale a business. You've read all the books and have all the information (files), but your life still looks the same. You're busy being busy and you're starting to feel burned out and get getting (processor is overloaded). You just want to make more money, but you can't seem to figure out what's wrong. You think you know what needs to be done and you "kind of" do it, but deep down you feel yourself pull back when things become "real" and you have to do actions that don't feel like you. They scare you just enough to make you pull short.

So, you don't fully take the actions and, therefore, don't fully get the achievement or reward. You blame it on other people, the market, having too much to do, etc. (the programs are the problem). You might even blame it on the fact that you don't look a certain way or you're not in good enough shape (the hardware).

The truth is that even with a great body, a powerful brain that doesn't get overloaded, and all the information in the world, you cannot have success in life without the right up-to-date programs installed and running at their full potentials. You cannot properly run those programs at their full potential, with everything else in place, without the right identity in place, which means you need to have an up-to-date identity to have success in your life. You need to upgrade how you operate to elevate your life.

The biological computer that you are is only as successful as the operating system running it. Your identity. If you've ever felt stuck or like you should've had more success by now, then I believe the issue lies in your identity, and it needs to be upgraded—an upgrade that happens through an identity shift into your *"ideal"* identity.

A LIFE ELEVATED

Here's an intimate share that is an example of a core upgrade I personally made to have a marriage as strong as I do now. In my first book, *Trust Your Hustle Pt.1: A Life Forged By Fire*, I share a story of how my divorce unfolded. However, at the time of writing that book, I hadn't yet made the upgrade and wasn't aware of how everything had truly transpired. My marriage ended in a ball of fire after my wife had an affair.

At the time, I was obviously deeply, deeply hurt. I spent the next three years damning her at every opportunity and laying all blame on her while I bounced around from relationship to relationship, never feeling fulfilled or like I had any closure on how things happened the way they did. There are two side of this story, as there always are, and after remarrying my ex-wife and building an unbelievably amazing marriage, I have had the ability to navigate my own upgrade and see the fruits of that labor.

Here are the facts. I had lost a sense of identity at the age of 25 after my NFL career was ripped away and I ventured into the world to find my sense of self. I, unfortunately, neglected my wife, our four-year-old son, and our newborn twins as I tried to recreate my sense of confidence in a new identity. I was gone from 6:00 a.m. to 10:00 p.m., six to seven days a week, leaving her alone and without any help. Not mention I wasn't even making any money. I was at work trying to build something, and she was at home trying to keep herself and the family together. Alone.

She was in need of a husband who could fulfill her needs. And I was nowhere near living up to her expectations. So we slowly pulled farther and farther apart without knowing why. She hadn't ever experienced this level of stress in her life and was not equipped to handle it. She did what anyone in need would do. She found a way to fulfill the need. She did it in a way that was absolutely wrong, and we both agree on that, without a shadow of a doubt.

We were both at lower operating system levels. I didn't know how to handle the loss of identity, and she didn't know how to address and/or handle the internal pain she felt due to our situation. Neither of us had the neural capacity to make the "updates" and stretch into the actions necessary to fix our marriage. So, as any program without the proper update would do, it crashed. That crash was an ugly divorce with neither of us responsibility. The two of us blamed each other on multiple levels, failing to see our individual shortcomings and part to play.

Years went by. Then, somehow, we both separately but simultaneously upgraded our operating systems, hardware, and processors. These upgrades led to her realizing she made a horrible decision and no excuse could make it right. She understood she didn't have the identity at the time to navigate the situation properly, even though life was showing "update alerts" that she kept snoozing. She failed in her own right.

I understood that although she made a horrible choice, it took two people to get her to that moment when she made that choice. She had been blatantly telling me what she needed, but I was ignoring the alerts and kept snoozing them. I was still out doing whatever I wanted. I failed in my own right.

In the end, we were acting out of such low operating systems that we couldn't have handled things properly even if we were given the perfect circumstances. We each had to go out into the world and find our own ways of upgrading at an identity level. This led to both of us gaining the mental capacity to understand the situation differently and forgive each other. The ability to forgive rather than burning out and harboring anger is an example of expanded capacity. Our ability to upgrade how we operated has led to an elevation of life we both had no idea was possible.

REFECTION SECTION

Shift your thinking – What part of this chapter shifted a way you see yourself or the world?

Stupid shift – Where in your life can you see that you've been acting or doing thing with stupidity and are in need of an upgrade?

CHAPTER 3

YOUR IDEAL IDENTITY AND GAPS

The Oxford Dictionary's definition of "identity" is 'the fact of being who or what a person or thing is.'

I agree. However, I think the definition is missing an explanation of how your identity shows up in your everyday actions in life AS you are "being." Being as a verb, not as a stationary entity at rest. Essentially, how does your identity make itself apparent through your everyday actions in life?

My personal, "actionable" definition of identity is 'who you are and what you do when you are not thinking about who you are and what you're doing.' This definition came to me after unpacking some interesting science.

YOUR DEFAULT MODE NETWORK

Picture yourself sitting, like I am right now, on a sunny fall day, at a black wrought iron table in a public courtyard, surrounded by lush greenery and trees cascading over a pond with five-foot-high water geysers. Kids are playing nearby, and you can hear their giggles. You see a dog walk by, and a grin sneaks onto your face. You pan to look at the happy people nearby and, before you know it, you find yourself fixated on the sporadic but beautiful pattern of the water falling onto itself from the closest geyser.

Your mind unknowingly floats off, and after about 30 seconds, you see someone waving out of the corner of your eye. Embarrassed, you snap out of it and gesture to let them know you weren't looking at them but at the water geyser right over their shoulder.

In those drifting moments, when you weren't presently focused on the outside world, you'd actually gone internal. You were with YOU. We call it daydreaming. It's actually hard to put into words what was happening in those moments because it wasn't happening in a conscious manner. You had ventured into your default mode network, or DMN—a part of your brain where scientists believe your identity resides. This is a subconscious mental space that physically exists in the medial prefrontal cortex, posterior cingulate cortex/precuneus, and angular gyrus that houses your autobiographical information. Scientists are still studying these lobes in your brain, but they are coming to understand more and more each year. Who you ARE is inside there; it's the comp-YOU-ter running in the background.

It shuts down when you're consciously thinking about "who you are," like when someone asks who you are, but it lights up when you stop trying to describe yourself and your subconscious starts trickling through. It's seen in how you act, react, judge, etc., in a knee-jerk manner. When you're not actively running the things you do through a filter, you'll see your identity clearly bubble up to the surface.

In addition to these unconscious actions, many conscious actions that you take also spring up from your identity. Whenever you make a decision to help someone or not help someone when they have a flat tire could trickle back to your identity and whether or not you are "the kind of person" to be seen on the side of the road doing manual labor. Whether or not you apologize after statements made in a heated argument may be rooted in your identity based whether or not you see yourself as the kind of person who admits fault. Even identifying as a certain race or religion can impact the conscious choices you make to stay in alignment with that part of you, even though deep down you don't truly understand the reasoning. We live our lives, day in and day out, through conscious bias and beliefs that stem from our identities.

So, scientifically, you are who you are when you aren't thinking about who you are. This happens frequently when your mind is distant, but it also fires up when you get into highly emotionally engaging moments; when you're triggered and simply react. It's the operating system doing its job in the background and running the programs in your life autonomously.

BECOMING AWARE

Unfortunately, this happens far more often than we may think. It happens when you don't feel like making that call and don't, when someone pisses you off and you retort, when you don't want to do that workout and don't, when the imposter syndrome creeps in and you shut down, and so on. In those moments, past habits and mindset—"who you are"—kick in subconsciously and take action. Or they don't take action. In those moments, you are "being" as a verb.

There is this statement I love that goes, "You cannot see the label when you're inside the jar." I'm not sure who first shared it, but I am thankful they did. Right now you and I are living our lives in blissful unawareness. In fact, we're almost always unaware that we're unaware. We randomly trapse through our days without truly having much awareness of our identity and where it truly shines through and affects every nook and cranny of our life experiences.

The benefit is that you're not taxing your processing power or overloading your operating system most days. You're just going through the motions of your identity's common habits. Identity is an asset in that way; it preserves energy while also keeping you functioning and productive. With that in mind, all you have to do is consider what would happen if you could exert the same level of low emotional energy and system processing power but have a higher-level outcome so you achieve more with less stress and effort than you're experiencing now to succeed in life.

What is interesting is that you are programming that operating system ever so simply and "becoming" someone every second of every day due to the things you are doing or *how* you're "being." Think about it. When you never answer your phone, you're becoming that person who never answers their phone. When you can't control your diet, and you're being gluttonous; you are becoming an unhealthy person.

I don't want to mince words here. Every single day, you are being someone, and that someone is also becoming someone.

It's a continuous, simultaneous cycle that has always been and will always be present within you. It shows up in your big and consistent actions on a daily basis, usually without you even being consciously aware of it.

So who are you "being" and "becoming" right now?

A WORD ON HABITS

I think this is a good time to briefly address habits. We'll discuss them more later on, but I want it to be clear—habits are a HUGE piece of the identity-shifting puzzle. There are great books by great authors such as Charles Duhigg, Brendon Burchard, Dean Graziosi, James Clear, and BJ Fogg that I've thoroughly enjoyed and recommend you pick up if you want to really comprehend the depth of how habits are formed, from a scientific standpoint, and the power they have on your life. In fact, if you want to make an identity shift, it's borderline impossible without focusing on habit changes. Many of these authors discuss this fact, and I fully agree with them.

My goal with this book, however, is to unpack and clarify identity for you, not just habits; to give you a working model of identity that you can learn to adjust and upgrade if/when necessary to achieve your goals—the goals you have now and the ones waiting for you to set once you understand the greatness tucked away inside of you. I want you to understand how your identity was initially formed and how you can select the proper habits and attach them to your core identity drivers to shift into the identity of your choosing for the future success you desire. It's simply a matter of programming that operating system of yours so that your biological computer can experience life at a level far beyond your current comprehension.

Simply think about what you want most and the type of person, outside of your current self, who would be living that experience or having those "things." Now come back and take a look at your current self and all the things you have. Does it line up? If so, where did you develop the identity traits to have the things you have. Maybe you're hardworking, compassionate, focused, communicative, and diligent, so you've attained some great things in life. So where did that come from? TV shows you watched growing up, your parents, coaches, teaches, etc.? External influences helped build your identity during your formative years, and that's often why it shows up the way it does now. That, or you thankfully picked up new traits along the way.

We sometimes select habits for our lives without understanding who we'll become with these habits in the long run. Sometimes these are good habits, but they are not nearly as useful if they aren't intentional. Habits we acquire guide us to shifts in our identity without us realizing it. I want you to be able to strategize your habits differently so the outcome is not only increased achievements but also transformation into your intentional ideal identity. I want you to be able—for the first time, most likely—to craft who you desire to become by taking control of who you're being every day.

I bet if you go back to a point in time in the past, you'll be able to recall a new situation that landed in your life. You were directed to learn something new, try something new, say something new, respond in a new way, etc. This could have been in a new career, in a new relationship, after the loss of a loved one or a difficult failure, etc. Without even thinking too deeply, you should be able to recall something. Within that window of time, you had to reactively adopt new habits, actions, mindsets, beliefs, thoughts, and pride to move forward. My goal is to make that a proactive choice you forever and always get to make to take back control of your future like never before.

I remember clearly having to make an adaptation to my life when I decided to enter this world of personal development as a coach and speaker. I'd previously developed a habit of keeping my emotions and my story close to the vest. I didn't want anyone to know the truth about where I'd come from. I came to realize that hardship is a shared human experience and hiding mine would hinder my ability to provide the help I desired to give to the world. So I developed a habit of getting right to that moment where I would usually stop sharing the story, and I would instead let it come stumbling off my tongue.

This simple habit in that singular moment opened up a floodgate of new actions I took and habits I ingrained into my life. From there I went on to film and post a new 90-second video every day for 1,333 straight days, 3.65 years, without missing a day. This habit I adopted was me being different, and I became someone different along the journey. It's one of the foundational aspects of who I am today and what I can do because of how transparently I came to share myself and my stories, as well as the smoothness of delivery I developed. My "being" every day "became" someone who now gets paid to impact lives from a stage, a boardroom, or a video screen. This was something that previously outdated identity of me didn't have as a possibility. I made an identity shift, just as every single successful person you have every come to know has. If they hadn't, you wouldn't know their names now.

Your life is yours to command, and it's time to start owning, embracing, and loving this fact through your actions. It's time to stand up, take a deep breath with closed eyes, and slowly open them to the world under your feet and in front of you. It's time to start realizing that your dream reality is just a matter of intentionally planned actions taken and habits developed to upgrade your operating system and eventually shift your identity. It's time to connect your heart to the reason your lungs were given breath and BECOME that person to the depths of your soul.

To make that happen, we need to further explore the concept of becoming via being.

CONTROLLING THE SHIFT

In 1985, Lewis Carroll wrote a well-known book in which the main character made a very distinct statement that I guarantee you have heard said in a myriad of different ways throughout your life. These words may have actually escaped your lips at one time or another, but the weight of them was probably lost on you in that moment.

In life, we arrive at moments, like this one here, but we aren't presently reminiscing about our past. We're just in flow and "being" who we are without much thought about it. Then, if we're lucky, we get asked a very specific question that has the ability to change our perspectives and possibly our lives.

This character created by Lewis is Alice, and in the story, she was asked to talk about her recent adventures in Wonderland after returning home. If you're aware of the story, she is shrunk down and transported into a collection of experiences that would blow the mind of even the most seasoned LSD user. She answers with a statement that I believe has the power to change your perspective and your life. She stated, "It would be of no use to go back to yesterday, *because I was a different person back then.*"

It's as if the person she was before, who experienced all of those things, wasn't who she was anymore but a completely different version of her. She was somehow completely different yet still the same person.

This is the same way in which every person usually looks back on themselves when there's been a noticeable change in who they are and how they operate. If you were to google Alice's statement right now, you'd return 205,000 results in .47 seconds—results showing hundreds of thousands of people stating the exact same thing, referencing incredibly different experiences. Accounts of bad police accused of past actions who have remorse. Spouses who cheated on their significant others in the past but are regretful. Athletes who used to be burdens on their teammates and coaches but turned it around. The list literally goes on and on.

It's interesting that people don't say, "I had different habits back then," or "I had a different mindset before." No, they say "I was a different person back then." Now, I'm taking a very small jump to conclude that when people say "person," they're referencing who they are at their core—the foundation of who they see themselves to be beyond a habit and mindset level. It's at an identity level.

See, Alice "being" in those crazy moments while in Wonderland, without consciously thinking about it, then "became." The way Carroll wrote of her all the way back in 1865 was as a girl operating with curiosity, joy, fear, tactful words in heated moments, and many other characteristics. She did things that led her to *become* someone as things transpired.

Unfortunately, like the vast majority of our population, it was a haphazard, unintentional journey. She had no control of her environment and what it threw at her, and she poorly assumed she had no control, so she didn't take control of who she was becoming.

She just went with things, reacted unconsciously at times, and let the chips fall where they may. She never realized that every second she was acting and reacting was slowly solidifying her identity and who she would become, which made it seem to her like she wasn't even the same person at the end of the journey. She wasn't, which is actually the goal, but not in the unintentional, powerless manner she experienced. We, and she, always had the power to be in control of the programming taking place.

Just like Alice, we are always just rolling with the punches and hoping we'll land right side up somehow. We act and react unconsciously with little if any thought about who we're becoming along the journey. This has been going on since we were children, and the majority of this operational programming was solidified by our late teens. So we ventured off into the world with what we believed to be a set amount of processing power and a piece of hardware that couldn't be improved upon. That's why you'll find people in life who shut down at the sight of difficulty as an adult in the same manner they did as children.

According to famed psychologist Erik Erikson, we go through different psychological stages, what he calls psychosocial stages, as we progress through life. Each stage has different transitions, but during each transition, one will experience a crisis that can result in positive or negative personality development. Crisis in this context means an unexpected situation that leaves a person navigating a new problem without adequate emotional or logical tools at their disposal. Consider the infant who never gets consoled when they're crying and the lack of love and comfort they feel. The child whose parents go through an ugly divorce when they're five years old; they assume it had something to do with them, so they bear guilt and shame and develop a belief that they are a burden. The early teenager whose first love only dated them to get to their friend and broke their heart, so they assume they're worthless. The late teen who is thrust into a new world and drops out of college because it's difficult and they feel stupid and inadequate. Or the twenty-something that gets fired from their job and instead of taking it as a setback sees it as an opportunity to truly pursue their dreams without hindrances. Each situation can have a negative or positive association that gets programmed deeply into our identity, and sometimes we live out of that for identity our entire lives. It's this programming that can be responsible for positive or negative development. I don't want to get into a philosophical discussion about what would be deemed negative or positive development, so I'll frame it like this: Each psychosocial stage inevitably involves moments throughout life that create crises, which lead to the development of our identities. This identity, and how we operate with it, will bring us closer to or farther away from a more successful life, according to our terms of success, without us knowing it in the moment. Our actions and reactions craft our experiences, which craft our identities over time.

This is why hardship can harden or break some people. Or why having a smooth life can give you perspective and compassion for others or leave you with an undeserving sense of superiority or entitlement. It's not just what happens but also how we choose, or are taught, to process the experience that cements our identity over time.

Between the ages of 12 and 18, we go through the fifth psychosocial stage called fidelity and termed as "Identity versus Role Confusion." The way Erikson explains this stage is that individuals are faced with who they are and their role entering the adult world as an adolescent—their roles in career, relationships, society, family, housing, hobbies, etc. At this stage, we take who our identity has developed into up until this point and launch ourselves into the world, whether we're fully prepared or not. Our computer system has been programmed and we're expected to use it. We're left trying to figure out who we are while trying to simply survive the day to day. So, who we are eventually sticks, and we start operating from that state of "being" for the remainder of our years unless we upgrade our operating systems.

As we're met with a crazy unfamiliar world, much like Alice in Wonderland, things come at us quick and crazy. We're left unconsciously acting and reacting to what's going on around us, crafting our identity along the way without intention. We just operate in a flow, but that operation is almost never intentionally revisited and upgraded throughout our lives in accordance with the future we desire. So, as time passes, we periodically look back on our lives and say, "I was a different person back then" when referencing our past. We have grown, but almost never intentionally or with guidance. So we continue to fall short of an elevated life because we're trying to run new programs with an outdated operating system and a brain that's processing power hasn't been expanded to handle any new load.

Unfortunately, we usually say "I was a different person back then" in reflection on bad times we climbed out of, mostly because those bad times forced us to adapt unintentionally to a negative situation we landed in, and we adapted to these situations on the fly, with little critical thinking. If it is in reference to good times, it's usually because we find ourselves in a bad situation now. So, we adapt by making minor, on-the-fly upgrades to our identity, like eating better but without a real plan, reading a couple books but not knowing if they're the right books, or "doing the work."

All the while, we are still stalled out in life and hoping something will give.

So, as we're "being" and progressing daily to "become," we do so because we're unaware of what comprises our being. Just like a thermostat in your home, you can't adjust what you can't see—"unless you have an Alexa in your home," as my sharp-tongued booger of an 11-year-old son, Taurean, would say. I want to introduce you to the "thermostat" of your being. The levers of your identity that, when pulled, can be shifted at an identity level to change your life in any intentional direction.

YOUR IDEAL IDENTITY

Ideal Identity Venn Diagram

I've mentioned your six core identity drivers a few times now. When these powers combine, they fooooorm...Captain Planet! Sorry, I couldn't pass on the opportunity. They actually come together to form what I call your ideal identity. The perfect identity for your dreams. The identity you need to have in place and operating if you have any chance of experiencing the life you desire most. These drivers are actually in place and operating in your life now, but they're most likely not "ideal" for your dream(s) at the moment. These core drivers are your beliefs, thoughts, big actions, mindset, habits, and ego, and all of these operate inside communities with different social, racial, and cultural dynamics. These drivers all come together to create your working identity and state of "being" on a daily basis. **For a personal copy of the ideal identity chart head to www.IdentityShiftBook.com/resources**

These aren't just buzzwords that I'm listing off, though. They all come together in a unique configuration to fooooorm... No, I'm not saying it again.

All joking aside, they do, in fact, connect in a powerfully clarifying way, and once you understand how, you'll be able to clearly see the ways you can adjust each lever to fine tune your identity to its ideal position for your dreams.

Captain Planet! I had to...

I'm done with that, I promise. Now, having the ideal identity for your dreams is a powerful concept I need you to understand as we dive deeper into this. It's actually tied to a very logical thought process. You have dreams and aspirations. Those dreams and aspirations would already be yours and you'd already be experiencing them in your life if you were the person inside who has those things at an identity level.

Let me simplify that because we both need you to truly grasp this concept before we continue. Everything you have in life, right this moment, is there because of who you are and how you've been operating, "being," every day of your life. Consciously and unconsciously. If you're missing something or you want something more than you have, it's not because of some timing issue, the market, your lack of support, lack of resources, lack of insight/

info, or any other thing you may try to come up with to justify not having it. Nine times out of ten, it's because you're scared of, or apprehensive of, doing something. If you weren't scared, it would already be done. You're operating at an unconscious identity level below what's necessary for your dreams to be yours right now.

There is a higher version of you who can, in fact, operate in a way that has everything you want in life. This is what I mean when I say if you were already that person internally, you would already have those things externally. It's not an easy pill to swallow, but it's essential to accept this now so you can give yourself permission to upgrade. If you fight that reality, you'll be fighting to keep your limitations. I love what Gay Hendricks says about that in his book *The Big Leap*: "If you fight for your limitations, you get to keep them." So, don't.

Also, please do not take this to mean there's something wrong with you because there isn't in any way. In fact, I know people who are incredibly happy in life who operate far below you or I. The difference is that their goals and aspirations reside down at the level they operate from in their lives. They have joy because they don't desire more than they have. Your dilemma as an ambitious person lies in the fact that you have dreams and aspirations above the level you're currently operating at. This means that every day you're met with the realization that you don't have something you want, and what's worse is that you've been trying to achieve it with no or poor results while realizing that you're possibly the cause of your lack of success. This can be a pretty defeating feeling. None of this a problem, per se; it's only a problem for you because of what you want to achieve. However, it's a problem you can solve permanently.

THE SIX CORE DRIVERS

It begins by simply understanding the six drivers, how they interact with each other, and how you can adjust them to shift your identity and, in time, change your life. You need to understand how each individual driver ties to your identity. How each driver interacts with the others in harmony to create the identity you are operating with right now. Then how you can use that info to craft your "ideal identity." The ideal identity for your dreams in life.

Beliefs

Let's start with **beliefs**—what you believe about yourself, the world around you, what's right, what's wrong, and essentially any other area in life where you find yourself having a deep conviction. In my opinion, beliefs are the core of your identity. When you go out into the world on a daily basis, you're running from belief systems. Your belief that if you don't go to work, you won't get paid and won't be able to pay for your lifestyle. Your belief that the car stopped at the stop light isn't going to unexpectedly run you over when you cross its path. The belief that your kids are safe at school. Your belief that you are meant to do something incredible in this world. Big or small, beliefs are the root foundation of what allows you to function without freaking out at everything that could go wrong in life.

For our purposes, I want to focus on the last belief I mentioned because it is the most relevant to you achieving a specific set of goals in life. What do you believe your purpose on this planet is? On my *Aww Shift* podcast, I ask my guest a final question to prompt him or her to think deeply about that belief. The question is, "What promise did God make to the world when he created you?" The answer to this question should inevitably lead to the belief you have about why you're here and the calling meant for your life. It's this belief that drives me and every other person who has desired something greater than the status quo in life. If I didn't believe I was promised to you and this world to help you reach your full potential, I would have never put myself out into the world the way I do. Whether I have a predestined purpose or not, it's that belief that drives me. It's also the type of belief that leads you to become a great parent, athletic director, spouse, coach, business owner, etc. What you believe drives your heart. So what do you personally believe in so deeply that you'd fight for it?

Thoughts

The next driver is your **thoughts**, both conscious and subconscious. For the moment, we'll focus on conscious thoughts. Conscious thoughts are an offshoot of your beliefs because they are fed by your belief systems. Your beliefs inform your brain to start thinking about something in a certain way. If you believe the Earth is flat, you will absorb and filter information differently depending on whether the information aligns with your beliefs or not. However, thoughts also have a mind of their own because, well, you have a mind of your own—a mind that's constantly taking in new information and trying to improve; a mind that gets confused, spins off into La La Land, formulates new ideas, and questions everything, including the beliefs you have.

Our thoughts are constantly running, whether we are awake or asleep, and they tell us what we should and shouldn't do almost every moment of every day. We convince ourselves to do things using our thought processes. Thoughts drive us to take action or stop. They manifest as emotions, such as fear, joy, anxiety, happiness, confidence, apprehension, boldness, and countless others. What we think leads to emotions that trigger us to do or not do things. Without those thoughts in our heads, there's no telling what we'd do. That's why people with mental illnesses say and do things that catch us off guard. The thoughts that are driving their actions are vastly different than the ones we might have in a similar situation. That's why I'm such a proponent of getting comfortable being in your own head with your own thoughts. Fleshing them out. Understanding why you have them. What you're doing with them. What you're not doing with them. As well as what you could do with them.

Mindset

This leads us perfectly into one of the overlapping areas of the Ideal Identity Venn Diagram—the area where beliefs and thoughts overlap to bring the **mindset** driver to life. By now you should be familiar with the term "mindset." Mindset is a highly studied area in psychology, and Carol S. Dweck led the charge of bringing the concept into the mainstream with her book *Mindset*. In it she describes the difference between a fixed versus growth mindset. To simplify it, when one is operating from a fixed mindset, he or she feels that no matter how hard they, try there's no chance of improvement if they aren't capable of doing something right now. So, they shut down or repeatedly bounce around to new things, never pushing past difficulty to improve. A person with a growth mindset, on the other hand, feels that anything is possible, even when things are hard. They focus on improvement, no matter how far away they are from their goals.

The strength of the growth mindset is fueled by many things, two paramount ones being beliefs and thoughts. That's why the overlap here is so very important for having a strong, supportive, and actionable mindset. When your thoughts and beliefs are aligned, you can have a strong growth mindset that will propel you on to do great things. If they are misaligned in any way, you will struggle to create anything of consequence in your life.

Look at it this way. If you believe you're supposed to become one of the greatest athletes in the world for your sport (belief), but then you constantly tell yourself you suck, you're not capable, you don't deserve success, etc. (thoughts), that misalignment will create an incredibly weak mindset that will rip you out of the race to greatness before you even take your first step. If you believe you're meant to be one of the greatest trombone players to ever live and you're consistently affirming to yourself consciously and subconsciously that you're amazing, you're capable, you have what it takes, and that you'll overcome any roadblock that stands in your way, you'll create a powerfully strong mindset, which is capable of helping you grow into exactly what you believe.

This is why you need to have an alignment between your beliefs and thoughts in order to have a mindset capable of elevating your life. If you believe one thing but talk down to yourself internally, you'll end up watching everyone succeed from the sidelines of life, wondering why you never made it into the game in the first place.

Unfortunately, most people stop at mindset and think that's all they need to be successful. It's a critical piece of the puzzle but it's not the entire puzzle.

Actions

The next key driver is **actions**. Now, if you recall the Venn diagram, then you're aware that habits are coming up next, and these are a form of actions, so I want to make sure you get the difference between the two in this framing. Actions in the Ideal Identity Diagram are the big, bold, "needle moving" actions that have the ability to pivot your life on a dime in an instant. This is making the ask and closing the big contract, getting on your first stage, quitting the job, leaving the relationship, etc. Actions are the non-habitual big actions that have the ability to change and/or set the tone for the next stages of your life. These are a necessity if you're going to have anything better in life than you have at this moment. If you think back to any time in your life when great things happened, or really bad things, there was usually a singular action or event that led to it.

Successful people take those actions and elevate their lives while unsuccessful people pass on them, for a multitude of different reasons, and end up missing out or failing altogether. When you think about the things you want in life, there are going to be huge, scary actions you must take, far outside of your comfort zone, in order to achieve them. When it's part of who you are to take those big actions without fear, apprehension, or second thoughts, you separate yourself from the pack. Where most people may struggle to act on the first stage, you end up navigating hundreds of stages deeper, and success becomes normalcy for you. This leaves other people wondering how you do it and simplifying it as luck so they don't have to accept that they're not taking action at your level. This is why action is such a huge part of identity and elevating your life. You have to act past the fear and pain to create the life you want. You have to act past where you see your current identity taking actions.

Habits

The next driver is **habits,** and this driver sits at the intersection of your thoughts and actions. When it comes to who you are at an identity level, there's a common agreeance that you are what you habitually do. So, thinking about the things you should be doing to make progress, and acting on them consistently, leads us into your habits. We briefly addressed habits previously, but I want to make sure it's clear just how powerful and life changing habits are. The science behind habits is extensive and proves that habits run our lives. Some we consciously control, like the habit of getting ready for work in the morning, while others happen without you even realizing it, like scrolling on social media and snapping out of it, wondering where the last hour went.

Countless studies have been conducted on habits and how they show up in our lives, and it's clear that habits are what lead us into our identity. This is where the "being" shows up and you "become" someone. When it's who you are to do those things (habits), and they switch from conscious choices to unconscious actions, they amount to amazing output in your life on a regular basis with little energetic expenditure. So, you find that the actions to achieve goals become a part of your identity, and it's much easier to do things when it's who you are to do them. Achieving goals actually becomes who you are, and success is literally second nature. This is why successful people make the consistent habitual actions look easy. Success seems to flow with ease because the actions they have to take consistently flow easily for them.

I've found that far too many people have adopted habits of individuals they looked up to simply because they said they should. So you start running, eating vegan, doing CrossFit, etc., because someone else said it's helped them. Well, you're not them. You don't have their gaps, deficiencies, desires, family, beliefs, or current identity. That's why so many people get to the back end of a long phase of life and question who they are. They adopted habits and became a person they never planned on becoming because they created the wrong habits that created the non-ideal person. It could be the way they belittle their employees because their boss did, how they handle criticism from those who love them by getting angry instead of reflective, how they run red lights because their parents did. They never thought about what these habits would do and who they would turn them into. You must determine what your habits should be based on who you want to become because your habits will turn you into someone whether you like it or not.

Ego

Finally, we get to talk about the area that I think may be the most critical to your success because it shows up in the moments that matter most. I believe that the most important moments in your life are the ones you've prepared for that are at the edge of your abilities. The moment when you get to see who you really are and what you'll get out of life. This is the moment you have to sell yourself on why you deserve the job or the promotion. Why you deserve the contract and should be hired. Why you are the one who deserves to win. It's the moment where you either stand up and fight tooth and nail for what you deserve or you sink down and let it pass you by because you question whether you deserve it.

That moment has come and gone more times in your life than you know, and its outcome is determined by this final area. It's the overlap between belief and actions. What you believe and the actions you take with that knowledge. It's your pride and your **ego**. People fight for what they deserve but unfortunately, they don't believe they deserve much, so they fight for little, or sometimes to stay little. Why is that? Well, think of it this way. Have you ever known you were meant to do something, and you knew you were the person for the job? Maybe you believed something needed to be done for your health, like eating healthy or getting exercise in. How did you feel after the moment passed and you looked at the poor action you took or didn't take? You felt a little crappy, right? Your pride diminished, and your ego took a hit.

That feeling follows you around all day every day, and it affects your actions. You feel crappy, and your pride and ego feel fragile and undeserving because of what you've done or failed to do. So you don't stand up proud and fight for something great because you don't believe you deserve it. It's one of the worst things you can have existing within your identity because it trickles into everything you do. If you don't have personal pride and a positive ego, you don't have strong beliefs. You don't have positive thoughts. You don't have a strong mindset. You don't have helpful habits. You most definitely don't take bold actions. The actions you take when you know and believe you should take them can affect every aspect of your life. If these are positive actions, they create a positive ego.

"What's a positive ego?" you may ask. Well, we all hear about how horrible it is to have an ego, but I believe it's the greatest tool we have to become subconsciously successful against the odds life throws our way. While my ego has shown up in negative ways, such as being unable to accept my faults in situations, not taking useful advice, and not asking for help, that same ego had positive aspects that have changed my life. My ego made me a great NFL linebacker by making me study my playbook, eat healthy, sleep regularly, lift weights, and show up every day with a focus on improving. The ego has an incredibly important place, and it shows up to protect your identity with actions. I call it an ego armor.

I see my ego as an armor around my identity. Your ego will protect the identity of whoever you see yourself to be because of the beliefs it has based on the actions you've taken. Unfortunately, it can also protect a crappy identity. That's why people think of the ego as a bad thing. You see it protecting narcissists by discounting other people's opinions. Protecting criminals by justifying their reasoning for committing crimes. Or by protecting people who self-sabotage because they have such low egos they think they deserve the pain they have in their lives. All because every time they promise to get better, they fail, and their ego and pride shrinks little by little. Their ego armor is protecting that crappy identity and keeping it stuck.

However, that ego armor will also protect the positive part of your identity with actions. If you're a good parent, then it will easily take the action of sacrificing for your kids. If you're a good boss, then you'll easily treat your employees well and do your best to help them do well with your actions. You believed in something, and you took the proper action; therefore, that is your identity. That is who you are, and your ego wouldn't let anything happen to your identity. You'll effortlessly take the actions necessary to maintain the integrity of who you are. Your ego and pride fight for you without you consciously knowing it.

When I was 15, I believed I had what it took to be a great player, and my ego realized I needed to do the actions necessary to embody that to my core. I decided I was a great player. So I did what great players did—lifted weights, ran routes, caught footballs, etc. Little by little, I became a great football player internally at an identity and ego level because I took the actions I believed

I should. Then, unconsciously, in every single play, I refused to let anyone take what I deserved from me. Success was mine because I earned it in the dark moments when no one was watching. Again, you will settle for nothing less than what you think you deserve, and if you build up your identity and ego, you'll protect what you deserve in the moments that arrive and leave before you even know it. In the moments when only your identity is present at an unconscious level.

CLOSING THE GAP

These six core drivers come together to form our identity, and when you want to elevate your life, you have to think about who you want to be in each area; the ideal person you need to be to achieve your goals. Hence the name "ideal identity." Picture that same Venn diagram of the ideal identity turned onto its side with propellers placed on each of the six areas. If you turned it on, and all six propellers started spinning quickly, then the entire structure would rise up quickly. However, if for some reason any one of the propellers wasn't going as fast, or if it wasn't working altogether, the structure would tilt and not be able to climb, and it would drift off sideways and crash somewhere.

That structure is you. Those propellers in your life have most likely not been spinning at the right speed, or at all, for you to rise to the level of your dreams at an identity level. You've been drifting off in odd directions and struggling to fully climb to the heights possible for your life because your beliefs, thoughts, actions, mindset, habits, or ego aren't elevated enough to bring your life to your next fitness, financial, or family goals.

You need to shift into that ideal identity, and there's a simple way for you to look at doing that. It starts with realizing that you are experiencing a gap. In fact, it's an identity gap. This is the space between who you are now, the things you're consciously and unconsciously doing, and the things you have and the identity version of you that has all the things you desire most in life. Picture a large hill with you standing at the very bottom of it. At the top, you see yourself, but it is a version of you that exudes another level of confidence and charisma. A version that has the things you want most in your life. There is a noticeable gap between the two of you, and in order to get what you want most, you have to climb that hill and close the gap between those identities.

When you're living your life with a gap, you'll feel it every day because you're reminded in everything you do of the fact that you don't have what you want. The gap shows up in your feelings of envy, anger, frustration, and sadness. You want something so badly and you don't have it, and even worse, you don't know how to get it.

The goal of this book is simple: clarifying how to close this identity gap so you can elevate your life to the next level. Like the title of this book says, you have to upgrade how you operate. Upgrade all the areas of how you do things at an identity level. Things that will return value to your life. We need to shift your entire identity to the ideal identity for your dreams and close your identity gap by upgrading and elevating YOU.

REFLECTION SECTION

Real Shift – Which driver stands out as the one you need to focus on most at the moment?

Hard Shift – Which driver do you think will be the hardest for you to shift?

CHAPTER 4

HOW YOUR OPERATING SYSTEM IS RUNNING YOUR HARDWARE

I was 14 years old, and I'd traveled with my best friend Jason and his family to camping grounds that were east of the San Francisco Bay Area we called home. The place was called Pinecrest, and there was a large body of water in the middle of the property called Pinecrest Lake. This beautiful lake sits in the California mountains and has a postcard view of lush green foliage and bright sunny days. Now, Pinecrest Lake is a decent-sized body of water, but it's not large enough to water ski or wakeboard. You aren't even allowed to actually bring any motorized vessels onto the lake. So, visitors rent out paddle boats and small outboard motorboats if they want to go out on the water and fish or just enjoy the open water feeling.

If you were to take a hike around the left side of the lake and follow the walking trail, which is beautiful, I might add, you'll happen upon a tucked away spot that leads directly out to the water. However, this direct access to the water is not a serene beach of any sort. It's a direct 20-foot drop off the side of a cliff. I remember the first time I went to this cliff with the intention of jumping off of it—and being deathly afraid.

The walk over was already taxing enough because the thought of it made my skin crawl. All I could picture was me not jumping out far enough, hitting the rocks, breaking my neck, and not making it home to my family. When we arrived, a ton of kids were all having a blast, jumping into the water, and so, like everyone else, Jason and I made our way towards the edge. Now I like to think of myself as a fairly tough person, but at 14, I was probably all of about 140 pounds soaking wet and, like any kid, I could scare the crap out of myself by simply letting my mind run.

So, I finally got up the courage to take my place in line, and my mind started spinning like a top.

Anthony, you're not the kind of kid who jumps off a cliff.

What if you die and never make it home?

All these boys and girls here, who you don't even know, are going to laugh at you when you look stupid.

DON'T DO IT!

Before I knew it, the line had dwindled, and it was my turn to jump off that cliff. I remember walking to the edge and peering over the side to see the water so far below that my heart stopped. All of a sudden, my feet became glued to the ground. I couldn't move, and every ounce of my body was telling me not to jump. I could see all the people down below treading water, beckoning me to make the leap with smiles on their faces.

What are those psychopaths thinking? I thought to myself. *Who willingly throws himself off a cliff?*

In my head, I wasn't the kind of person who did this sort of thing. I didn't believe I would be able to jump off this cliff and survive. That's why all the voices in my head were screaming at me to back away and ignore the voices of the other kids telling me I would be just fine and that it'd be fun. I edged closer and felt like a crazy person with every passing moment on that edge. Eventually, I decided I was not going to kill myself on accident and backed away from the edge.

That action of backing away made it clear to me that I wasn't going to be jumping that day. I let the person behind me go. It was my buddy Jason, of all people, who propelled himself off that ledge like a crazy person. I sat there looking at everyone else having a blast in the water below, and an instant wave of embarrassment and shame crept over me while I stood there on a rock so hot that I had to put my sandals back on so I didn't burn the bottoms of my feet. It was clear to me that I wasn't the kind of person who jumps off of cliffs into bodies of water.

Want to know what's crazy about this situation though? I wanted to be that kind of person. I wanted to be hanging out in that water with the cool kids down there. To have no fear of jumping off that cliff. To be the cliff-jumping kind of person that they all appeared to be. However, no matter how much I thought about it and tried to run it through in my head to gain the confidence to jump, I kept getting stuck on the fact that I just wasn't that kind of person. So I sat there and watched everyone else, who all had the same knowledge as I did, seem to have a blast while I slid back into the background and did the best I could to just not be seen while they all had fun.

Then, something happened. In a moment of frustration, I stood up, kicked off my sandals, got back in line, and found myself once again at the edge of my fears. I had zero confidence that I could successfully jump off this cliff, but I was tired of thinking about all the things that could go wrong. In fact, I was tired of thinking about everything altogether. I shut of my brain for a split second, and the next thing I knew, all I could physically feel was my stomach full of butterflies moments before cool water covered every inch of my body. I couldn't breathe for a second as I plunged deep into the water after the impact, and the wave of fear I experienced transitioned into astonishment and then excitement as my body floated to the surface of the lake.

I wiped the water from my eyes and looked around at a bunch of unknown people clapping and whistling for me having finally joined them in the water. I felt like I'd just won a world championship or something. I was now part of the cool kids' club of people who had jumped into the water. Before I knew it, I was climbing back up the rock wall and going for my second leap of faith into the amazing waters below. In fact, before the day was over, I'd completed probably over 30 more jumps, and what initially was me jumping in feet first had turned into me jumping off backwards, doing cannonballs, spins, and, at one point, I even did a flip. Yes, me, the kid who wasn't the kind of person who jumped off cliffs at the start of that day. I was now a cliff diver.

From that point on, I've always thought of myself as that kind of person the one who could at least jump off a cliff or a bridge into water. In fact, I no longer fear it but instead find it genuinely fun. Now, what if I told you that I've jumped off hundreds of cliffs in my life that had no water below them? I know you'd probably ask: "How high were the cliffs, and if they were high, then how in the world are you still alive and able to walk?" Easy. The cliffs I've jumped weren't actual rock cliffs but emotional and action cliffs that scared the crap out of me to begin with.

THE LEDGES OF LIFE

The first time I suited up for a football game in youth sports, I was deathly afraid of getting hit and getting hurt, but I eventually played in the NFL—with my hair on fire! When football ended, I was freaked out when launching my first business. Now, part of my business is teaching other people how to launch their coaching and speaking businesses. I was scared about being a young father in college, and now I feel incredibly confident about the fact that my kids will be able to raise great kids. I was worried that as a black foster kid I would be shunned as an adult for growing up poor in an all-white family, I wouldn't fit in, and I wouldn't be respected, but now I carry a weight of respect in any room I enter. I was ashamed and scared to share my personal story or teach lessons from my life as a "dumb football player," but now I can confidently speak on stages in front of thousands of people at once and write my thoughts down in books, like this one, which will live forever.

All of this goes beyond gaining and/or having confidence in these areas; it's who I am as a person to do these things now. It's effortless, and now if I'm not doing things like this, I feel off. Yes, things that used to scare me to my core now bring me joy. Think about your life right now. What are some things you do now with joy and confidence that you used to be deathly afraid of?

Maybe you're a parent. Maybe you've been promoted to a position that you're amazing at but once feared you weren't qualified for. Maybe you lost a relationship and thought you'd never find love again, only to be in a great loving relationship now. You might even be in business, running a company that started out as an idea that scared you to fully pursue. Regardless of what it is, there was a point where you were looking at a cliff that scared you, and you saw all the cool kids down below living out the lives you wanted, and you were deathly afraid of doing what it took to take that leap and be like them, but, one day, you did. That's why you're now swimming in the success you have.

Not only that, but you now self-identify as that person who deserves the success you have, and life wouldn't feel right if you weren't doing, or having, that "thing" in your life. How do you go from not even considering you deserve or are worthy of something to being able to fight to the death to defend the fact that you do? Where do people, all of a sudden, get than depth of ownership, confidence, and identity that literally changes their lives? Well, the answer is that it does not happen overnight, and it only comes from a hard-fought journey where investment bias is built. A bias that you do deserve something because of the investments you've made past the pain to earn the right to feel ownership.

You and I both know one truth, however. You have another cliff you've been looking at that you haven't been able to jump off of just yet. You're looking at another group of cool kids living the life you want to live that you can't seem to get yourself to jump into. Maybe it's a higher-paying career that you don't feel 100-percent confident pursuing. Maybe it's a new business opportunity that could pay off well, but the fear of risking what you have and losing everything is keeping you stuck watching others have success. Maybe there's a person who you'd love to be in a relationship with who doesn't know you have feelings for them. Maybe there's a dream that you can't seem to get out of your head but you can't seem to pursue either. Where in your life are you standing on the edge, not feeling capable of taking a leap into your next level? You've done it before, so why is it so hard to do it again? Why can't you take that next-level leap and finally achieve the higher-order goals you have sitting inside your heart?

THE LIFE MASTERY LOOP

The answer is you've been stuck in a mental cycle that is, and will forever be, perpetually running in the background. I call it the Life Mastery Loop—the actual processing path of your mind at all times. Where you're Ideal Identity shows you the core drivers that make up your identity, the Life Mastery Loop shows you your identity in action. Now while you may notice some of the same names from the core drivers within the loop (beliefs, thoughts, actions), they don't function in exactly the same way in this framework. The core drivers are the snapshot descriptive aspects of your identity, kind of like nouns, whereas the loop shows the traits in action, kind of like verbs. It's the difference between saying "horse" and "horsing around." What's unique is that these models feed off each other because the traits in action (the verbs), program your identity (the nouns). One is being while the other is doing. Then, the one doing programs the one being.

Throughout this chapter, I've actually already unveiled this framework in my story of jumping off a cliff, but you would have no way of noticing it without explanation. That's because this Life Mastery Loop happens to be a seamless flow that is so normal and natural to all of us that it goes right along without us even noticing it happening. This is how your operating system is functioning on a day-to-day, moment-to-moment basis.

This Life Mastery Loop is a powerful system to understand because it holds the power to change everything. It's the actual process you can manipulate to upgrade your operating system in real time to elevate your life. Something you can do through action. Something I actually hid inside the story of me jumping off a cliff. When you understand exactly what was going on in my head during those moments, you'll be able to dissect your own life processes. You'll gain clarity over why you may be stuck at a certain level of success in your life. Not only that; you'll understand how you can climb that wall and press on into greater success.

Life Mastery Loop

So let's dig into this Life Mastery Loop. You'll see from the graphic above that it's represented by a seven-step circle, which starts at the top and, for our purposes, works itself clockwise around. **You can get the PDF worksheet of the Life Mastery Loop at www.IdentityShiftBook.com/resources.**

IDENTITY ANCHORS

The first step starts with your identity, or identity anchors. Your operating system always begins out of the place that you currently see yourself. If I were to ask you who you are, you'd rattle off a bunch of statements that put your "self" into a box. That box is the structure with which you flow into the world. Whether you see yourself to be a lover or a fighter. Smart or stupid. Bold or scared. It doesn't really matter what you actually see as long as you understand that you do see yourself as "someone," and that someone you see is the starting point to any functions you have in life. Unfortunately, some people have an identity programmed in opposition to their goals and they perpetually fight a losing battle because they never realize they're unconsciously starting from a poor perceived identity every time they pursue something.

Beliefs

The identity you have leads to the next step in the loop—beliefs, or better, believing. In my opinion, beliefs are one of the most powerful things we have because they can power some of the most beautiful and most disturbing actions in humanity. Soon you'll see exactly how that happens. Beliefs are the core of our operating systems, past identity, because they set the foundation for which we see the physical world. Whether it's believing in something we've seen, or believing in something we've never seen, our beliefs tell us things about ourselves and the world around us, functioning as a filter.

If I identify with being a very wealthy person, then my beliefs about myself and the world will stem from that. I may believe that I am better than other people. I may believe I am entitled to certain things in life. I may believe that I can do no wrong. I may believe the world owes me something. On the flip side, if I identify as a poor person, I will have different beliefs. I may believe I am not worthy of nice things. I may believe I am less than other humans. I may believe I'll never have financial success. I may believe the world is a place that's scary and bad. These beliefs completely permeate our lives without us ever knowing it, almost as easily as a fish never really realizes it's in water. It's just the norm. In fact, they're programmed into us at such a young age that we never question them throughout our adult years until we're presented with this reality. Like you are now.

This believing locks us into a direction that many will continue for a lifetime without checking or adjusting out of fear of losing their compass—even if it's an incorrectly pointed compass leading to a troublesome place. We fear loss of the familiar so much that we even fear the loss of something we would benefit to lose. Beliefs can be amazing for our lives when they are positive, powerful, and helpful. The issue is that beliefs can be problematic for your future if they're rooted in a poor identity. Like many, you've possibly been fueling your beliefs with a negative identity that leads to being invisibly stuck without you even knowing why. This is why so many people struggle with their belief systems, improving them, and finding confidence by believing in themselves. The way to change a problematic belief doesn't come from focusing on the belief itself; instead, we must address the identity that is fueling the belief system in the first place.

Thoughts

Next comes the thoughts you and I operate with every moment of every day. We have an average of 2,500 to 3,300 thoughts per hour, which equals tens of thousands of thoughts per day. These thoughts, as you clearly know, are incredibly powerful aspects of how we function. The thoughts we have drive so much of everything we become, or fall short of becoming, in our lifetimes.

We have two different levels of the mind. One level is the subconscious mind and the accompanying thoughts that lead us like blind mice following a tune. The subconscious mind triggers unconscious thoughts, which show up as the emotions of fear, anxiousness, joy, etc., and these emotions will direct us into places in life that may hinder us from achieving desired outcomes. We will redirect our actions based on these unconscious thoughts simply because something we "can't put our finger on" doesn't feel right. The subconscious mind is heavily affected by our belief systems, as is our conscious mind. However, the subconscious also fuels the conscious mind. Throughout our day, the conscious mind is driving the direction we go, and it leads to the actions we take and don't take, along with the vigor of those actions. The less vigorous, powerful, and bold the actions, the lesser the outcomes.

Feelings

This leads us perfectly into the next stage of the Life Mastery Loop: feelings. These feelings of ours are truly special things. Feelings are the things that we understand but don't understand. Things that we can control but can't control. Things that I am unscientifically calling "things" at this very moment because they're so difficult to truly anchor down to a simple description. These feelings we have are a rollercoaster within our own bodies most days. Then, we add on the navigation of others' feelings, and it becomes a twisted mess of crazy most of the time.

All of your feelings are fueled by your thoughts. See, your thoughts, conscious and unconscious, become the catalysts for your feelings. In fact, the subconscious mind is the primary reservoir of feelings outside of our conscious minds. That's why If I think I am powerful, I have positive feelings. If I think I am weak, I may have feelings of fear and sadness. Many people walk through their lives having feelings running through their bodies that seem, to them, impossible to get under control. In fact, I know many people who simply write off their feelings as things that are wildly out of their control, forcing me to have to just deal with their capricious mood swings. It drives me crazy because I'm well aware that it's not an impossibility but a lack of desire to take control. They're instead letting themselves be dictated by a source that they aren't even trying to understand in the slightest. Then the world has to deal with the craziness that is their life. Feelings are not uncontrollable entities that live within your body, however. Feelings are a controllable force that can do good or do bad, and that control is always within you. It's not always easy, but it is possible when you address your thoughts.

Now, if you factor in what we've already unpacked, you can already see the flow of identity—from beliefs, to thoughts, to feelings—and start to make more sense of what's going on in your life. If you identify as being a bad person, you likely believe you aren't worthy of good things, which leads to thoughts running in your mind on a daily basis of how little you deserve because you're a bad person. That immediately leads to feelings of lack, less than, and possibly sadness. If you identify as a good person, then you likely have beliefs about how good you are and the possibilities the world holds for you. You have positive and uplifting thoughts that lead to confidence and feelings of strength. It's incredibly interesting to me how simple yet complex we are as beings.

Actions

Now, getting back to the loop. The next step is the one that becomes a life changer. Actions. In our world, the only way anything happens is through actions. Not intentions. Not ideas. Not planning. Actions alone are capable of building a better life. Actions alone are capable of upgrading your operating system. It's the action of placing that cold call that can grow your business. The action of saying "I love you" that takes the relationship to the next level. The action of running that helps you get in better shape. The action of making the "big ask" that moves the needle for something important. People fail to comprehend the simplicity of this fact and the power it holds. At the base of everything is a truth that the only thing separating you from where you are now and the next level of what you desire is simply a collection of actions.

These actions you take are fueled by the previous levels. Your identity leads to your beliefs that drive your thoughts. Thoughts that turn into feelings. Most importantly, it's the feelings that directly trigger your actions. If you feel bold and confident, then you take bold and confident actions. If you feel unworthy, incapable, or scared, then the ensuing actions won't happen in a bold manner.

Now ask yourself this: When in your life have you taken poor actions that resulted in something incredible happening for your life? I can't recall a single time personally, and that's the law of actions in effect. I don't believe we should be rewarded at a high level for when we don't take action at a high level. It's your actions, and your actions alone, that have the power to change your life. As long as you take actions below the level your dream demands, you don't have the right to be upset when you can't elevate your life.

Outcomes

These actions we're speaking of immediately take us into the next stage of the loop, and your life. Outcomes. Any time an action is taken, there is an outcome. Some outcomes happen immediately while some take time to manifest. Accepting the promotion now returns in an immediate betterment of your career. Placing a call to get someone on an interview may return in the "yes" you've been hoping for. Pressing the remote turns the TV on now. Working out is an example of an action taken over time that returns a desirable outcome farther down the line. It's these outcomes, fast or slow, that we experience as our lives. When you think of powerful memories, they are born of these "outcome" moments in life.

Environment

The next part of the loop is your environment, which is the most living, breathing, experiential part of the entire loop. Once an outcome takes place in life from an action taken, you receive an immediate feeling that fuels the creation of your environment. Your environment includes both your internal environment (how you feel about yourself) and your external environment (what your physical world looks like around you). When you have the "yes" outcome happen after you've taken the action of making a big ask, your internal environment of pride swells and is beautiful.

If you got a no, then your interval environment withers and you feel angry or insecure.

Your external world will start to adapt as well. When you get the "yes," you may make more money, increase your community of support, have more notoriety, and even more income to change your quality of life. If you get a no, then you stay stuck in a lower experience of life—less friends, less money, less influence, and a lesser life experience. These environments are quite literally our day-to-day experience of life and they are charged by all of the previous loop levels.

These environments inform the ending and the beginning of the entire Life Mastery Loop—your identity. The way you feel inside about yourself and the physical environment you see around you tell you who you are. Your environment tells you whether you are or are not a worthy person. It tells you whether or not you have the skill sets, success, or reasoning necessary for your goals. Now, whether you are right or wrong is a different discussion, but the fact remains that you inform yourself more and more about who you are as you experience life on an internal and external basis.

The crazy part is that this loop is always spinning. Until now, it's been running in your life without you realizing it. In fact, this is exactly what people talk about when they describe self-perpetuating cycles because who you see yourself to be leads you down a path to solidifying that day after day. This is how the stories you tell yourself come true by your own making. If you say "you're stupid" to yourself, you'll continuously run the loop and solidify this for yourself, even if you do not want it to be your life.

If you don't identify as the person who has that new career, then you won't believe you're capable of getting the job. So you'll let your mind wander off into negative thoughts that do more damage than good. This leads to feelings of doubt, fear, anxiety, sadness, and a desire to escape the interview you have scheduled. So, you show up to the interview with those negative emotions driving your actions, and before you know it, you're sitting in a chair fidgeting, and your entire demeanor is unsettling to the interviewer. Your answers come out with a shaky voice and an apparent lack of confidence. The interviewer can feel your unease and uncertainty, so they lack confidence in your ability to properly do the job. Then, you get the "not at this time, but we'll keep your resume on hand" outcome. This leads to a poor internal emotional environment—one that confirms your initial identification of not being capable or worthy. This also leads to having an inability to have an improved external environment. Your outside world ends up matching your inside world.

On the opposite side of the coin is the person who identifies as being amazing and deserving of success in the interview and getting the new job. This person believes they are powerful and capable and that they have what it takes to succeed, and if they don't, they can find a way to get past any roadblocks. Their thoughts are positive and uplifting at all times, and they control them so there is only space for the positive. This leads to feelings of confidence, power, capability, and vigor.

So, the actions they take in the interview exude that power and confidence through their body language and their voice. The interviewer enjoys this and feels at ease hiring this person for the job, so the outcome of the interview is, "Congrats, you got the job!" This creates an internal environment of elation and accomplishment, which leads to more notoriety, income, impact, and a better physical experience of life. This leads to a confirmation and even upgrading of this person's identity as being the person deserving and capable of their next level of success. Again, their outside world begins to match their inside world. Then the wheel continues to spin uphill for them.

Life is an odd machine in this way, and the better understanding you have of this loop, the better you can manipulate it to manipulate your life. However, you're probably asking yourself, "How do I shift this loop from the way it's running in my life right now to the way I want it to run?" Great question. While I wish it was easy, I have to be honest and tell you that it's not. It's far from impossible though. It starts by looking at each step within the loop and figuring out which steps are most adjustable in a way that will have the greatest impact. If you try to change your beliefs, you'll notice that it's incredibly difficult without having a slight shift in identity. If you want to adjust your thoughts, you'll find it is somewhat possible, but it becomes difficult if your beliefs haven't been adjusted; your old beliefs will just trickle back into your head, little by little. You can try to change your feelings, but if I'm being honest, that's not the easiest thing to do if your thoughts are always against you. You can try and change your outcomes in life, but that's almost an impossibility if you fail at taking the actions necessary to create new outcomes. You can try and change your environments, but that's beyond difficult if you don't have outcomes that fall in line with your desired environments. You can try to simply shift your identity on a dime, but without the rest of the loop running the proper way, it is impossible for your identity to just randomly shift.

The answer lies in a small space tucked between your feelings and actions. As much as I've tried to find another spot that can have a greater impact on your ability to adjust the loop to run in a more beneficial way, I have yet to find a better solution. Think about it this way. If you simply started by taking a crazy, bold, and powerful action, what would happen? Well, you'd have a great outcome, which leads to a better environment, which would lead to anchoring a positive identity. If you didn't yet have a positive identity, the new environment would call the accuracy of your identity into question and inform you of something different—and better—being possible. It would then lead to a new set of beliefs to fuel your ongoing thought processes, which would lead to powerful feelings and another set of powerful actions to elevate your life perpetually. So, you understand how the actions are the key to literally any life change you want to make—I already mentioned that—but now you should be able to fully understand why.

But what if you don't have the feelings necessary to fuel those powerful actions? Well, it's actually quite simple. This is where you'd have to step in and do exactly what I did as a teenager who was considering jumping off a cliff. You'd have to take an unconfident action that's completely out of line with how you feel. Like me shutting off my brain and just making that leap.

If you're being honest with yourself, you know it would not be the first time it has happened in your life. There's a 100 percent chance that you've done something you didn't feel like doing and just said "F it" and did what needed to be done. When you do that, you actually activated what I call your secret self—the self inside of you that can rise to the occasion for a moment and do what needs to be done in a bold manner, no matter what crazy emotions your body is experiencing. You let that "self" take an unconfident action in the direction of your dreams, let the loop stay in motion as it does, and watch the aftermath of amazing take place.

When I was a kid, this is the exact process I went through that took me from fearing death by jumping off a cliff to doing flips off that cliff in just a matter of hours. Over that period of time, I became a cliff jumper. Yes, there were some reps where I failed and belly flopped, but I kept getting up and taking action against my fearful feelings to create that version of me. It's the same process I went through when I decided to make a shift into this speaking, coaching, and writing industry of personal development as a thought leader. I didn't identify as that guy but I kept jumping off that "cliff" by taking the necessary, unconfident actions every single day and, over time, I became this person. As I mentioned previously, I filmed and posted a video called the Nightly 90 every single night for 1,333 days—3.65 years—just to develop the skill and confidence I knew I needed to have an identity rooted in this profession. There are no shortcuts. It takes work and it takes time. However, simply knowing this process should provide you with a clear picture of how to accomplish those goals that have been just out of reach.

This is exactly how you have arrived at the life you are living right this moment. Any large leaps you took came from simply stepping into a bold action that was taken against the momentary fear you felt. Taking the test. Asking for the phone number. Launching the business. Handling the negative feedback. Signing the big contract. It's always been there, and it must happen again, at a higher level, for you to reach that next level for your life. You need to find that next stage and set your sights for it. Arrive at the moment where your emotions are setting up to shut you down. Then, activate your secret self and dive fully into that next step to create the shift in the self-mastery loop necessary to achieve your goals.

Living a better life isn't about finding a quick fix for success; it's about finding a path to your purpose through a worthy adversary capable of giving you the confidence and pride to puff your chest up and own who you now are. It's about understanding the deeper reason why you will go through the necessary pain to achieve your goal. Most people go their entire lives without knowing how this loop is running, and they give up far too fast. They don't realize that it simply takes a repeated effort against the emotions that are slowing them down. It's continuously taking the bold steps that will inevitably lead to a complete overhaul of one's life's experience.

So, I want to help you get started on the path to elevating your life far beyond what it is. Unfortunately, most people don't take bold actions without a catalyst moment. A moment they can look back to and reference as the big reason they made the choice to finally make a change. So here is your catalyst moment. I am challenging you to think of the scariest bold action you can take on this very day that you know, done long enough, will adjust the spin of your loop and shift you into your ideal identity. If anyone asks you why you finally decided to make a change and take a bold action, just tell them Anthony Trucks challenged you. So, what are you going to do today?

REFLECTION SECTION

Shift Comes Around and Goes Around – How would you rate your current Life Mastery Loop level in terms of success,1 being it's low and 10 being it's the best it could ever be?

Bold Shift – What is the bold action you will start taking?

PART 2

THE SHIFT

CHAPTER 5

THE SHIFT METHOD

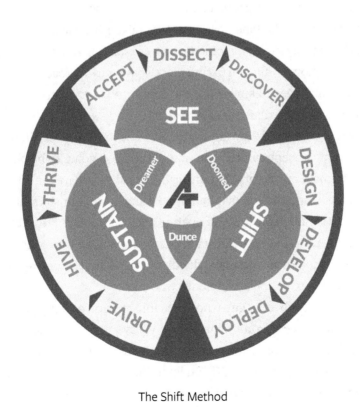

The Shift Method

I want you to think back to a time when you were starving. All you could think about was getting your next meal into your mouth. The thought of savoring the flavor of that meal quite literally made you drool. Put your mind back there for a moment, and let's say, a chef shows up to make sure you get fed. You see the chef walk in with bags of ingredients, prepared to create your favorite meal.

The chef walks into the kitchen, places the bags on the counter, and then walks over to you and starts telling you how he's going to make the meal. He goes in depth about the type of seasoning he's going to use, how he's going to use the utensils, the temperature he's going to cook at, and continues on and on about the concepts of cooking and how great the meal is going to be once it's finally finished. All while standing in front you, talking instead of cooking. In thinking back to that moment you were starving and visualizing this situation, I want you to consider two ways to approach it. You can let him keep talking about the concepts. Or you can tell him to just create the damn meal already.

My goal in the following chapters is not to simply stay in the realm of concept and tell you how great life is going to be once you've made an identity shift. Instead, I want you to have the actual strategies and tools to take action now and make your shift real— to actually upgrade how you operate and elevate your life. We're now transitioning into the realm of creating this shift in your life. Those who are able to make the distinction between desire and dedication to action are the ones who succeed.

I've always been a guy who loves information and my ability to attain success from it, but the only way I attain success is by application of what I know. So, be prepared to now start the work that will change your life. If you let it. I'm about to teach you the method that I've come to develop from over three decades of life experience, years of scientific research, tens of thousands of client conversation hours, and hundreds of thousands of dollars invested in education and experiences as well as a ferocious desire to help people like you make a shift in their lives.

One of my fondest "post shift" memories took place in 2019. I sat quietly in a chair alone. Eyes closed. The pulse of the three-foot-tall subwoofers that lined the stage climbed up through my shoes, all the way up my spine, to the crown of my head. The tingle tightened my skin and created a wave of goosebumps that excited and oddly comforted me. I was about to grace the stage in front of three thousand people who were amped and ready to absorb all that I was about to give them.

As I was getting introduced by the host, I finally felt it.

I never seem to get that wave of anxiety and nerves until the very moment I hear them start talking about me before showing my entrance video. Most of the bigger events have projector set-ups where I can watch the video in reverse from the backside. It never fails to overwhelm me with an emotion of realization. A realization of how vastly different my life could have been based on all the things life has thrown at me.

At this moment, however, I was in deeper gratitude, literally watching my life unfold right before my eyes. This moment wasn't different from any other moments like this one, except for the fact that I let it in deeper. I had fixed and strengthened my marriage into something unbelievably amazing, and I had just got off the phone with my wife, who gave me the "atta boy" to go kill it on stage. My kids were happy, healthy, and doing well in all their academic and sports endeavors. My business was making income and impact at levels I never thought possible. I was in great shape and in awe of the crazy things I'd accomplished that were playing on the screen—like me hitting a buzzer on *American Ninja Warrior.*

As I saw the video reaching it's end, I heard the host's voice come back on the mic and boom across the entire room. "Welcome to the stage...."

In that instant, every ounce of me felt a wave of power build up, ready to explode out past the stage curtains.

"Anthony Trucks!"

Now, in this moment, most people would think the nerves hit an all-time high. They'd be wrong. It was then that they immediately shifted from anxiety to pure joy and excitement. It's as if the emotions get so charged and powerful that they have no other place to go than out as you step out into three thousand sets of eyes and hearts prepared to take you all in. This moment is seared into my mind because it was the culmination of so many small and large shifts over so many years to bring me to a place where someone not only trusted me with that many of their people, but their people also trusted me to give them something in that time I was about to take out of their lives. I delivered for both in stunning fashion.

After an hour, when I finally got off that stage, it finally hit me: I was quite literally not the same person I was seven years before that moment, who didn't want to be on the planet anymore. This life I am living seems like a dream that I hope I never wake up from. What elevated my life to this level was what the method I'm about to share with you. If you desire your own moments like this, all you have to do is follow the method. Now, I'm well aware that you may have no intention of ever gracing a stage in front of thousands. However, you may want to become the best manager at your job. The best leader to your company. The best in your marriage, parenting, or whatever you heart desires. That is all possible when you make an identity shift INTO that person

There's a powerful future just beyond your fingertips, just waiting for you to access it. The Shift Method I'm going to unpack for you gives you the key to peek into the doorway of your future, right before kicking the door in like the Kool-Aid man and stepping into the biggest room in the world—your room for improvement. That room is where you will make the greatest shift in your life—into the life that you deserve to live and that's anxiously awaiting your arrival.

The Shift Method is my gift to the world. My gift to you and everyone else who is willing to make the effort to make the upgrade and achieve any goal they've ever wanted. By breaking your dream life down into achievable action steps and taking those actions, you will make the greatest identity shift in your life. By taking action that is consistent and sustained, you will achieve levels of life beyond what you've ever dreamed is possible for you. You can head over to www.IdentityShiftBook.com/resources now to get a free worksheet on the Shift Method.

The Shift Method is something I wasn't aware existed until I looked back at my life and the life of every other successful person I'd ever known. I've always heard that success left clues, and this is a clue that I finally picked up. It started when I personally heard multiple people say they were "a different person back then," referring to a time before they were successful. This led me to look back at my life with a microscope in a way I hadn't previously considered. I noticed that every time I was in a rut, and struggling in life, and I wanted to achieve a higher level of success, I was applying this method. I noticed that every life story I uncovered from other successful people had the same through line. I wasn't alone in this process but, like everyone else, I hadn't noticed the writing on the wall. So I spent years doing things the hard way and accidentally applying this method. When the light bulb came on and I saw what was going on, it led me to view my life in a whole different way.

The stages I had been going through were simple. I would see into myself at a level I hadn't seen before. I would also see a new opportunity that inspired me that wasn't present before I noticed what was holding me back. Then I went into a phase of working towards it until I achieved it. A process that took time and energy past what I initially thought it would take, but I stayed the course. Finally, when I achieved that particular successful outcome or level of success, a sense of pride would be engrained in me with regards to the sets of actions it took to achieve that level of success and sustain those habits. That sense of pride would function to not only maintain that level but go beyond.

There are three phases involved in making a life-changing shift and upgrading your operating system to elevate every part of your life. You have to see what's going on, make a shift, and sustain your work in the direction of your dreams. Most people skip to the Shift Phase, which is the work, but they end up working tirelessly to achieve a goal and pop their head up one day to notice that they're dead tired, dead broke, and feeling dead inside with no motivation. It's like they huff and puff to climb a ladder leaned against a building and, as soon as they get to the top, with sweat dripping down their face, they make a stark realization. The ladder is leaned against the wrong building. That's why we start by seeing, then head into the work to make a shift, and finally sustain that course to success. It may sound simple, but making a true shift is anything but.

SEE

The first stage of the Shift Method is the See Phase, and I want you to truly see it for what it is. The See Phase examines two very critical areas of a person that few people ever peer into over their lifetime. The first area is your blind spots. The areas of your life that you fail to notice because they aren't made visible to you—the way you carry yourself, the way you handle hardship, the excuses you make, your snap judgments, your optimism or pessimism... The list could go on and on. These are the parts of your operating system that are so second nature that you've normalized them and it's become your default setting to live with these limitations.

Everyone else can see your issues; however, it wouldn't even cross your mind that anything is "off." These blind spots are the invisible walls and chains holding you back from success; they're keeping you stuck. It's when you can't seem to figure out why you're unable to get the promotion, but everyone else knows that it's because of how you carry yourself in meetings. You think you do a job great, but, privately, everyone sees that you're not. It's how you never seem to get anyone to buy your products or services, and you think it's because your script is off, whereas everyone who is hearing your pitch knows that you don't seem to believe in the product from your demeanor. Not to mention that you cringe at the mention of certain tactics that are recommended because it "just isn't who I am to do that." We call those identity walls. Walls that you can't/don't climb because it feels out of alignment with who you are. Even if it's something you really should be doing, for example, people who don't work out because, "I don't exercise," or "I'm not a gym rat," even though it's incredibly helpful for your health.

So, you keep on working on the wrong things, or nothing at all, and wonder why you're still stuck where you're at over time. The chains of your identity are keeping you stuck, and the identity walls stop you, even if you are to unhitch yourself from those invisible chains. You're blind to see the real issues swirling around your life and, therefore, any work you do keeps ending in you falling short of your goals and potential. The best chance you have at solving this issue is being able to deeply reflect on, and SEE, who you are truly being every day that is becoming this person. I am also a huge proponent of enlisting people close to you to help you see things that are hidden in your blind spots. You just have to be able to take the tough love meant to give you clarity so you can create something better that's capable of getting you past your identity walls.

The second area you need to SEE is the end destination that draws your heart to it. A bigger vision and dream. Whenever you live your life with blind spots, you limit the distance you can dream. We all dream at a level that seems attainable to us at that moment. We rarely dream of something we can't see as possible. That's why I don't get up dreaming of winning the Tour De France or an Oscar this year. I don't see either of those as remotely possible in this current identity, or at all honestly. If the level you're dreaming up to isn't inspiring because you don't think you can attain much, then you never even consider taking the first step. However, if you do manage to take a step forward, you stop at the first sight of strife or struggle. Those chains are keeping you limited from the very beginning, and you're oblivious to it. You just keep on chugging right along, doing the same things over and over, hoping that something will eventually give. It won't.

So, in order to make any forward progress, you need to first see what's in your blind spots. What's really stopping you. The problem is that few people enjoy doing this. Let's be honest, though, how many people like being told what they're not good at, or areas they can improve, even if it can help? I personally don't know many. Even athletes who get harsh feedback every practice, which can and does help them, don't enjoy it. Most people will vehemently fight to justify their position so they don't have to take ownership of their failures or lack of success. They'll place blame externally and resist internalizing anything to save face. This is that oh so annoying ego rearing its ugly head again. This is why it's genuinely Everyone's Greatest Obstacle because the first step to any improvement in life is SEEING. What you can see you can improve. Unfortunately, you cannot see what your ego won't allow you to look at. Hence the reason so many people never fix what's truly broken in their blind spots.

Once you are able to see what's holding you back, you can see what's possible. I have a Blue Nose Pitbull named Tonka. He's a great dog. He's lazy around the house, but the moment we hit a field, he will legitimately run himself into the ground pure excitement to be free. It's interesting to watch the transition from leashed to free take place in his eyes. One moment he is tethered to me by a leash, which he knows only allows him to travel a certain distance from me.

He's excited about being outside, but he stays close because he doesn't feel like being choked by his collar and leash. Then I stop, lean down, and remove his leash—and wouldn't you know it. He's still sitting next to me. It's not until I give him a final smack on the butt that you see his eyes finally shoot up and open as he realizes that he's free to run. In an instant he SEES what's now possible and, he's off like a bullet out of a gun for the next 15 minutes. Once he's loose, you can barely get him to even come back to you because he's afraid you'll put him back on the leash.

Now I mean no disrespect by making a comparison between you and my dog, but we are all like Tonka in life. Unfortunately, we don't regularly run, or dream, at full speed like he does. We start out with dreams that may excite us and make our hearts race—kind of like driving down a straight open road, a cool desert highway, in a cherry-red convertible Ferrari with the pedal to the floor and the cool wind flowing through our hair. The way we'd feel about that moment is the same way we usually feel about our dreams when we first have them—hearts beating out of our shirts. Now imagine that you're driving that Ferrari and, all of a sudden, you see a speed bump or a wall. You'd have to slow down and anxiously move past this annoying obstacle before you can start speeding up again. But then you realize there are a lot more of them. It's no fun. You might as well get out of the car.

These speed bumps are the equivalent of what happens in life when you're dreaming and you start thinking of reasons why your dream cannot or will not happen. You're not dreaming at full speed because you're creating your own speed bumps and retaining walls that kill your passion to pursue greatness. You're like Tonka when he's stuck in place and not even seeing what's possible. So, you lethargically wander around life, devoid of true passion because you have no idea how to get off the leash, or if you ever will.

The moment you decide to remove your invisible chains and walls, you'll realize you're off the leash. This feeling is unlike anything you can imagine until you've actually felt it. Just like Tonka, you'll finally be able to SEE, with excitement, what's truly possible to explore. Then you can finally run full speed towards your dreams and be in joy.

I just hope you aren't reading this section like it's some pipe dream that's not possible for you because it is. There is no reason you should believe that the next level for your life doesn't exist. All you have to do is figure out what your personal leash is. Keep in mind that it's usually hidden behind your ego, which is busy protecting the identity you have in place now; protecting your feelings from pain of the realization that you may be to blame for your lack of current success.

Once you do finally remove those chains and see what's truly possible, the world opens up into something beyond imagining. Quite literally. There's a great quote by Dr. Wayne Dyer that says, "If you change the way you look at things, the things you look at change." Such a powerful and true statement. The new perception you have creates a space to literally see the world in a different light. What used to hold you back now becomes a propellant for your life. The perceptions we hold on life are powerful drugs that, in the right doses, can kill or inspire our dreams.

I like to take dreaming one step further once I have personally seen what I believe I can accomplish. This is when I commission individuals I know who are at higher levels than me, or see me differently than I see myself, and know me well enough to provide insight. I ask them a simple question to extract insights on myself. "What is a dream I should consider that you know I haven't seen yet?" It's this question alone that has spawned ideas that have stolen my soul. Ideas that make my heart swell at the idea of achieving them. THOSE type of dreams are what spark the drive to move forward with vigor and passion. Dreams that were beyond my imagining before I removed my chains and identity walls in life.

One of these extractions took place in 2016, when my wife found what I call a "pinky finger power" of mine. Something you have as well. We had just returned from living in Costa Rica, where, after three short weeks, we had to make an immediate escape back to the United States. When I was headed out of town for a speech in San Diego, there was a kidnapping attempt on my children at their private school. Yes, as crazy as it sounds someone in Costa Rica saw my family as a target and made an attempt to kidnap my children and hold them for ransom. I rarely talk about it because my heart hurts at the thought of what my life could have looked like if they succeeded.

The rekindling of our marriage was just as fresh at this heinous experience. With an obviously rocky situation still just outside of our minds, we moved home so quickly that we had to live in a small two-bedroom apartment in our hometown while we looked for a place to live. My wife, in all her splendor, decided she'd secretly fill out a TV show application for me for a show called *American Ninja Warrior* in October 2016. She mentioned it briefly without fully explaining it, and she filmed some random videos of me at the gym where I was doing pull-ups with weights around my waist. I thought nothing of it, and it left my mind as fast as it had entered.

Fast forward to February 1, 2017, and I'm sitting at our small kitchen table in this two-bedroom apartment. My phone rings, and an unfamiliar but excited voice on the other line informs me that I'll be competing on national television in just four short weeks. I had totally forgotten about this show, and, at the time, I was 240lbs and in no shape to be hanging by my hands on TV. I had no visions of this. I had no belief I could do this. I'd never even seen this show before. She had dreamed beyond what I thought possible. When I saw what it was, which is pretty much going through a brightly lit, red, white, and blue obstacle course from bar to bar by your hands, and over balance tests by your feet, in the middle of the night, in front of a national audience, it flipped a switch in me and thought about how cool it would be to hit a buzzer on this show on TV. To accomplish something that seemed borderline impossible. I got genuinely excited, and the dream pulled at my heartstrings. Four weeks later, after digging deep, training, dieting, and preparing my mind, I showed up to the Universal Studios lot in Los Angeles, prepared to take on the obstacle course.

It was 3:00 a.m. on March 6, 2017 when I traversed six crazy obstacles and became one of the first former NFL athletes to hit a buzzer in the show's history. I even banged my head on one of the apparatuses and almost fell off a balance obstacle before saving myself by doing the worm. When I hit that buzzer and the smoke poured out, as I looked down at a screaming crowd and, more importantly, my wife and kids, I was overcome with pride and excitement. I was counted out by the producers, who had laughed at the thought of me hitting the buzzer in the pre-show interviews. I was counted out by the announcers, who, early on in my run, mentioned that big guys like me never make it. I was counted out by my own brain early on. The person who did not count me out was my wife. She anchored me to a vision beyond what I could have ever imagined and she led me to believe in her belief. Something that changed my life.

I am positive that in your years of life you have come across a dream that sparked your heart's fire. I have more times than I can count, to be quite honest. The problem is what typically happens after that dream has been lit on fire. It's the stages that call upon us to invest actions to bring the dreams to life. This is where the "shift" hits the fan. When you now have to look at the journey you must embark on to realize that dream. Let's be honest, also. The path looks treacherous. There are obstacles you've never encountered littering the path. You have no idea if you'll make it there alive. Essentially, this current identity is seeing what must be done and throwing up in its shoes.

I get it though. This is where the choice is made to move ahead or not, but this is where you find out the key to always moving ahead. It's making an identity shift. Plain and simple, that is the key. This moment is where you are given the opportunity to upgrade your operating system through action and take on the challenges ahead. This is where you must download the updates of what must be done and upload them into your life by the actions necessary to succeed. This is where all those files and strategic information you've accumulated over your lifetime become assets, but only if you actually put them to use. This is where you shift.

SHIFT

Which is why the second phase is called the Shift Phase. Now the Shift Phase obviously works best when you have a clear vision and dream in mind that you want to achieve. The focus at this stage is tied to that dream, but it's not the only thing you should be focused on. The Shift Phase is focused on who you will become through your actions of being throughout the ensuing days. The planning during this phase is all about your day-to-day being that will allow you to become the person who is capable of operating at a level to have the dream you've envisioned. You have to have to upgrade how you operate to elevate your life to that level. Without an upgrade, you may find a way to achieve your dream, but you'll arrive drained of your willpower, with marred relationships, out of shape, or with a person you don't know or love—a version of you that you didn't plan on becoming because you were only focused on the achievement and took no notice of the transformation inevitably occurring. Sound familiar?

In the Shift Phase, the goal is to plan out the actual steps to take to achieve and transform simultaneously. I do mean simultaneously. See, most people only work on one aspect during their stage of growth in life. They focus on achievement and neglect the transformation taking place—100 percent focus on what they want and what it takes to get it, with 0 percent focus on who they are as a person while pursuing it. They never stop to think about the fact that they are transforming into someone every day, whether they like it or not, as well as the fact that without a focus on transforming, they'll actually shortchange their true potential for achievement. Think about it this way; if I want to achieve the goal of weight loss (achievement) without adjusting my internal attachment to crappy food (transformation), I'll have to kill myself in workouts to lose that weight, and I'll get burned out while also negatively affecting my goal of weight loss the entire time. This is why you have to focus on transformation while achieving.

The reverse is true as well; you have to have a focus on achievement while trying to transform. There are many people who will shut down their lives and tuck themselves away with the intention of making a personal transformation. They spend time in their heads thinking through breakthroughs without taking any actual action. While there are situations and circumstances that do give this strategy its own level of merit, I have found that in order to truly transform inside, I need to do something outside. When I wanted to become powerfully confident in myself and develop self-love, I couldn't do it while sitting in a chair trying to convince myself. Those massive transformations came when I dug deep, poured my heart out, and was proud of myself through the actions I took to achieve a desired result. Actions that reflected back to me what I was truly capable of when I pushed past my limits. Things that created that internal sense of pride and transformation that wasn't possible until I achieved something special.

My earliest experience with this phenomenon was back in 1998. I started tackle football at 14 years old, after being adopted and finally being allowed to play the game. My peers had all been playing for as many as seven years more than me, which left me at a vast disadvantage due to the skill set level alone. All my years I had watched these guys come to school in their cool jerseys and wanted to be them. I'd demolish them in recess, so I knew I had some ability to play the game. When I finally stepped on that field and tried to play with a helmet and shoulder pads, they demolished me. That joy I'd had to play was stripped from me faster than a peel from a banana. The realization of how bad I sucked and how much it hurt to get hit caused me emotional pain. After that season, I contemplated never suiting up for the game again and hanging up my jersey at 14 years old.

My friends and family talked me out of that idea, and I chose to play another year as a freshman in high school. I got to a school where I was for the around people of my culture for the first time, but I felt like a fish out of water. My adoptive mom had been diagnosed with multiple sclerosis, and it had shaken my family. My older brother, in a family of six kids, who was my rock, had taken off to the military. Not to mention all of my friends I'd had since second grade had decided to attend another high school. I was lonely, floating through life in a very troubled state of mind. Life was very fragile at that time. I tried my hand at finding myself in sports, as football was something I still really loved, and went full out into that area of my life. Lo and behold, I showed up to freshman year and...I still sucked. The ever-so-poignant pain of being tackled and getting told I sucked came flowing back in like a tidal wave.

By the end of that season, I had decided I was utterly and completely done with this game. This is the same moment I shared in Chapter 1 about the statement that girl made about being so bad because she was in foster care—a statement that was profoundly unsettling because I never wanted to be the person who would say that. That statement shifted my heart when I had all but given up. After she shared those words, I lifted weights, I ran routes, I caught as many footballs as possible, I started learning the plays, and every other thing you can imagine a great football player would do. I continued these actions even when my teammates made fun of me for it, saying, "Trucks, what are you doing? You suck, bro!"

I committed to doing all of those things before I knew I would be successful, even with ridicule. Reread that last statement. It was a commitment to doing what it took to be great without a promised return of actually being great. It's the investment all must make but rarely do. Then they wonder why they fail. What I did not realize was the true return I was going to receive from that investment and how it was so much more valuable than I could ever imagine.

Every day that I was out there putting in work, I was focused on creation—creating a stronger, faster, more skilled physical body capable of performing at a higher level on the football field. I was going through the arduous process of getting up and working on days when I wanted to stay in bed. I completed my workouts even though I was sore from the previous day. I skipped fun activities with friends to keep my commitments to myself. I was making sure nothing got in the way of my goals. It started out difficult, but somewhere along the journey, it got to feel so normal that I felt awkward even thinking about skipping something.

Doing those things was becoming who I was at a deep level inside. I just kept pushing, and the harder I pushed, the easier, and more fun, it actually became. I had this sense of self that grew with literally every single rep I took. After an entire offseason of this, I showed up to summer workouts my freshman year, still a scrawny 160-pound twig, but I was an ANIMAL. It was in those moments that I drew on the investments I had made. I had no idea that the rate of return was 10-fold mental over physical. The entire time I had been creating this physical body capable of performing at a higher level, I was also creating a set of intangibles at an identity level that were vastly stronger than my body.

When that ball was in the air, it was MY ball—no matter who it was thrown to. When someone was running away from me, I thought they had to be out of their mind to even think they could get away. When I had the ball, I was disgusted at the thought of someone bringing me down. A little crazy, I know. There was essentially a complete 180 in confidence, self-esteem, desire, and every other necessary intangible you can imagine. I was no longer a kid trying to play football. I was a football player. The intensity I had on every play came from the fact that I had invested far too much in the dark, away from the public eye, that it was impossible for me to not collect on what I deserved in the light. It was my new identity to succeed, and you had better not dare try and strip me, of it or I would fight you to the death.

It was in that year I came to embody a statement that would change my life. A truth I wouldn't come to truly know for almost two more decades.

What you create creates you....

See, I had shifted my identity through a set of actions taken difficultly against every ounce of who I saw myself to be at that time. Those actions, over a long journey, have effectively led me to these words right here. Those actions were a process of actual creation. When you think about creation, it's a long, arduous, dirty, grueling path of baring your soul to bring forth something you can only see in your heart and mind's eye at onset. Creation is just plain hard. Think about Michelangelo creating David, Elon Musk creating SpaceX, or even you creating your life. It was all hard, and at the end of a creation, not a single person steps back, looks what they created, and says, "I suck and I'm not a <insert identity here>". Michelangelo was a SCULPTOR. Elon Musk is a WORLD-CHANGING ENTREPRENEUR. You are a MOM, DAD, FRIEND, COACH, ETC.

You become who you are through the actions of creation. You cannot have two identities fill the same space in a given area. You can have multiple identities, such as one at work and one at play, but you don't have two at work. Those creation actions drain your soul of who you used to be so they can fill your soul with who you are now. It's a gift you must earn through the hardship of creation; through the action that must be applied to make a true SHIFT in your life to become, do, and have more in all areas. This is a gift of identity, emotional, time, and often money returns that you have to realize comes at a cost—a cost that you must pay if you want to achieve the dreams you tell the world you want to achieve.

So, you either need to get into your head what it's going to take to achieve your dreams or get the dreams out of your head.

SUSTAIN

The final stage is the Sustain Phase. In this phase, the goal is simple. To sustain the trajectory you're already on and sustain the climb to even greater heights in life. If you go through the incredibly difficult process of upgrading how you operate to elevate your life, why wouldn't you do everything in your power to make sure you don't backslide? As simple as that question sounds, I see it happen every day. People do very specific things to achieve great goals only to stop doing the things it took to get to that level. Before they know it, they're waking back up in their old life or an even worse one. I wondered how and why this could ever happen to someone, and the reason became apparent when I spent time with people on both sides of the success spectrum.

On one side, you have people who use willpower as the fuel to achieve their goal, and they burn up every ounce of energy they have to accomplish their goals. They cross the finish line dead. This happens when a person feels like the things they're doing aren't "them," meaning they are forcing themselves to take the actions and of a different identity to win. Their "processor" is running two identities (their true identity and the one necessary for success), and it gets to the point of overheating. These types of people literally do not have anything left to keep up with the actions necessary to sustain their success once they have it. They burn out and shut down.

On the other side of the spectrum, you have the person who is keenly focusing on becoming the person who does the actions necessary to succeed. This person doesn't try to work out; he or she is the type of person works out. This person doesn't try to be a good spouse; he or she is a good spouse. This person doesn't try to build a successful business; he or she is a successful business owner. The actions that take place after you identify as someone great happen with far less of an energy drain. When you identify as that person, the actions come from a desire to be in alignment. DESIRE. When you desire something, it is a fuel that fills while it burns. When you achieve success after having made an identity shift, it's far easier to sustain that level of success, and the extra stores of energy can be allocated to achieving even greater success.

In this stage, you focus three simple things to sustain: your **drive**, your **hive**, and the extent to which you **thrive**.

Your **drive** is the extent to which you are still motivated to succeed in the direction you are aimed. This is a check-in that saves lives, marriages, careers, businesses, and so much more. You may find that if you no longer have the drive to succeed that you have inadvertently made a U-turn back to where you began.

Your **hive** is the collection of humans around you. Like a beehive, which has a grouping of individual beings that work together to make sweet honey, I think our hives allow us to come together to create a life that is just as sweet. I do not believe that we are the average of the five people we surround ourselves with; I believe we are the *expectations* of the five people we surround ourselves with. In order to be sure those expectations are the ideal ones needed for our sustained elevation, we have to do two things. One is to remove people whose expectations fall below the level our dreams demand. These people may actually be as successful, or more successful than you, but if their expectations aren't high enough for you or for themselves, they don't fit. The second is to add people to your hive who have the expectations necessary to elevate your life to your next level. These could, in fact, be people that are below your level of success, and in my opinion, that's sometimes better because their drive can be infectious.

The honest truth is also that this hive can and should always be a fluid life process. Some people come and go in life, and that's OK. Some people aren't meant to be around forever, but they serve a purpose for that season. Some people do, in fact, hang around much longer because, in my opinion, they grow their expectations right along with yours or beyond, and that keeps you both on a sustained trajectory to greater things.

The final stage of the Sustain Phase is **thrive**—the act of existing in a place where you flourish. I have always desired to be in a place of pure abundance. I now often pause to take my life in, and the joy I sit with literally makes my heart feel so full that it hurts. It's a great kind of hurt. Hard to explain, but it's something I relish and want more of. It's something I want more of for YOU as well. This is the point at which you are able to continually sustain a direction of greater achievements without guilt.

Once I had great success, I realized that I wanted joy, but I didn't know exactly how to attain it. I could keep working and being happy, but I was missing that feeling of pure elation. I found it in giving, and it led me to a greater realization for all of us. Think about being the hungriest you've ever been and having 10 hamburgers. You eat the first one, and it is more delicious than words can describe. Your joy levels rise. You're still hungry, and you want more, so you eat another one. It's still delicious, but since you're not as hungry, eating it doesn't result in the exact same feeling as the first. The joy is there but slightly diminished. Your appetite still isn't sated, and you still want the joy that comes from eating these hamburgers, so you decide to start eating a third. Halfway through, you can't take another bite. You're full but you still want joy. What do you do?

Well, the answer is actually pretty simple. You find another hungry person and share the remaining seven hamburgers with them. Two hamburgers in, they feel the same way, and the two of you find another person to share with, and so on. By the time your meal is over, you're not only full and full of joy beyond what you can handle, but you've created that same feeling for three or four other people. You have a full belly and a full heart. All you can think of at this point is how do you get more hamburgers to get more of that feeling.

This is what thriving feels like. You have so much abundance that you want to give it to others. You have to take a look at yourself and SEE what is in your way and what must be done to accumulate more "hamburgers" in your life through higher levels of achievement. The entire process of the Shift Method perpetually continues on in this manner throughout your entire life if you choose.

This book is one of my "hamburgers" in life that I am sharing in the hopes it creates a higher level of success and joy for you, which I hope you may choose to pass on.

In my early life, when I was hurt and angry after being given away, I didn't have anyone trying to do this for me. I realized I could either take all of the pain I had experienced and do my best to cause more pain in the world out of spite and a desire for retribution or I could find a way to give what I never been able to experience to others in my relationships—the feeling of joy being passed on. I knew that I could never give what I didn't have, so I first had to get it for myself. I saw this firsthand from my adoptive mom in how she loved me past my crazy as a child. If I had it, then I would be able to pass it on.

This is why I made two promises to my adoptive mom right before her life ended. One promise was that I would get back on my feet in life and become the man she raised me to be. Then I would do as she did and unconditionally love others, regardless of whether they were blood relatives; I would provide the world with more of what it needed, not less. This Shift Method is that love I'm passing on.

REFLECTION SECTION

Wrong Shift – When in your life have you worked full speed and full effort in a certain direction, only to find it was the wrong direction?

Hard Shift – When have you worked incredibly hard on something, past what you normally would, to find a sense of pride and newfound identity as the kind of person who does that thing?

Good Shift – When have you sustained good actions for so long that you've actually been able to pass on the joy you've found to others?

CHAPTER 6

THE SHIFT METHOD: SEE

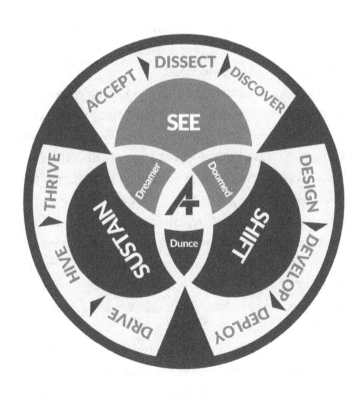

The next three chapters are tactical strategies to take action and make the most important shift of your life. The first shift. Whether you're struggling to find your first levels of success or you have already made your first million and you're on to your next, you are about to learn how to break through and clear a path to your most desired destinations in life.

It starts with the See Phase, which involves seeing where you are and where you want to go. In our identity shift coaching programs, this is the exact first stage I work people through. It's called Roots and Fruits.

In life we all have jobs we do to create abundance for ourselves, and this abundance is called the "fruit of our labor." When I first heard this statement, it sounded like a cliché and didn't have much impact on my life. As life progressed, I realized just how important it truly is for all of us to understand.

As we've covered, we all fight so hard to accomplish goals in life, and throughout this process, we become someone. However, as we become someone, we are always at the risk of experiencing a loss in life that leads us to losing that sense of self. When I was in the NFL and I lost that career to an injury, I lost a part of myself. I felt like I had lost everything. When someone leaves the military, loses a loved one, loses a job, a business fails, ends a relationship, or experiences any loss of something they've spent an incredible amount of time, energy, and money on, it feels like losing more than just that thing. When we're in these situations, we feel like we have lost a piece of ourselves. We feel like we have lost everything. We have lost the fruit of our labors.

At an identity level, in that loss of those fruits, the loss of something integral to ourselves, we feel like an apple falling from a tree and laying on the ground. We feel as though we have fallen from the tree's enriching source that gave us health and the ability to grow. The source of income, love, confidence, etc., is no longer flowing into our lives. Now, as is the case with the apple, it's not the end of the road to have fallen off the tree. Our sense of identity has a shelf life. Like an apple, it can fall off the tree, get picked up by a farmer, travel to a grocery store, sit in a pile, get purchased, and still stay fresh on the kitchen counter for a while. At some point, however, that apple will start to rot. It will eventually turn into a brown, soupy, worthless, rotten mess, and if someone were to consume it, they would get sick.

That's how we feel when we fall from an identity in life. For a while, we have the ability to give life and have energy; we carry that life-giving ability and confidence for a time period. At some point, however, that starts to die down. We feel just like the rotting apple—worthless and toxic. When my NFL career ended from injury, I left the game with a sense of confidence. I was fresh from falling off of the tree. I still felt like a winner. I mean, why wouldn't I? I was just playing football at the highest level in the world. As time went on, that feeling shrunk more and more by the day. The confidence-enriching source of the NFL was no longer there, and after being removed from that source for a year, I had lost all sense of confidence in my identity. I was a rotten apple.

Not soon after, my business started tanking, my marriage failed, I was out of shape, I wasn't a present father, and nothing that made me feel like "me" was intact. This is when life presented a message to me that changed my perspective and, in time, my life. In life, we always have thought, and felt, that we are the fruit, but you have never and will never be the fruit.

YOU ARE THE TREE.

Read that as many times as needed to get it to settle into your brain and heart.

See, the tree gave the enrichment to get me the fruit of the NFL, the fruit of my marriage, the fruit of my children, the fruit of my relationships with everyone in life, and the fruit of any material objects I owned. The tree is who I always was and always will be. When we identify as the fruit, we think it's all over when we experience loss, and we stop giving nutrients to the tree. So, not only does that fruit fall off the tree, our redirected focus on that single fruit detracts from watering the tree, pruning the tree, protecting the tree's soil and environment, keeping the tree in great soil/environments, and making sure the other fruit is healthy by taking care of the tree.

So, with no focus on the tree a neglected tree ends up withering, and, over time, the rest of the fruit ends up rotting and dying as well. That's how losing the football "fruit of my labor" in my life led to a dead marriage fruit, a dead parenting fruit, a dead business fruit, dead friendship fruits, and dead material fruits. Sadly, that one football fruit affecting all other fruits almost led to a dead me from the realization of so much loss and a desire to end the pain I was experiencing in this place.

This is the first step in making a shift, realizing that you are the tree and any fruit you have lost cannot and should not lead to a loss of other fruit in life. All you have to do is go back and tend to the tree that is you. When you do, you'll find, as I have, that you can produce bigger and better fruit in all areas of your life. Simply pruning dead branches, pacing the tree in the right environment and soil, watering the soil, removing unhealthy fruit from the branches, and giving genuine care to the tree can make for an indescribably amazing crop. When I finally grasped this concept, which, unfortunately, took me five more years of barely living fruit, I created and executed on a plan to bring my tree back to vibrant health.

I replanted this tree in fertile soil capable of enriching the roots, which was great friends and family who abstained from partying and drinking. I made sure to give the tree ample sunlight in the form of informational sources entering the body from positive places and watering it with the right fluids. This came in the form of people, news, TV, magazines, etc. All were designed to give the tree the positivity it needed to grow. This eventually led to a healthy tree with deep roots and abundant fruits. My marriage came back together after three years divorced. My business focus shifted and began to thrive. My children had a happy and present father. My health reached its peak since football, and I had so much "fruit" that I shared it with others to allow them to enjoy it. For some, those fruits planted seeds that have allowed them to grow their own amazing trees with strong and abundant fruits.

This is why I named this next stage Roots and Fruits. Once you recognize that your life is fixable and capable of being even better than it is now, you simply need to know where to focus that effort to establish great roots, which will allow you to grow abundant and delicious fruits. When a tree has deep roots, it can withstand the storms and rain of life. Picture a town demolished by a tornado with just a single sturdy tree in the middle of the chaos. When you have deep roots, you are able to withstand any storms and tornadoes life throws your way. Weaker trees are uprooted, get thrown off into the distance, lose their limbs, and are never the same again.

The Roots and Fruits Exercise is designed to measure the depth of your life's roots and the bountifulness of your fruits. You can head to www.IdentityShiftBook.com/resources to get a free worksheet to work through this process in real time for yourself. The purpose of this exercise is simple: to see where you need to focus your efforts in the Shift Phase.

Label each separately from 0-10 for how fruitful the area is or how deep the root is.

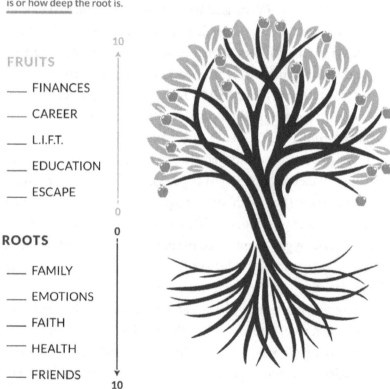

10

FRUITS

___ FINANCES

___ CAREER

___ L.I.F.T.

___ EDUCATION

___ ESCAPE

0

ROOTS

0

___ FAMILY

___ EMOTIONS

___ FAITH

___ HEALTH

___ FRIENDS

10

ROOTS

The first area we'll focus on is the roots because they are responsible for the depth and strength of the tree to withstand life's storms. They are also responsible for absorbing and delivering nutrients to the tree that can enrich the fruits. In other words, the roots allow the fruits to come to life and grow in the first place because a tree that cannot take root or absorb nutrients cannot create fruit in the first place. There are five areas I consider to be the roots of the tree of your life: faith, family, friends, health, and emotions.

As we progress, you will number each area for your life. When you're measuring each root, you can individually number them from 0 – 10. 0 being that this root has no depth in this area of your life; it has not rooted yet, and 10 being the deepest, strongest, and most powerful you can imagine this root being in your life.

Faith

Let's start with the first root: **faith**. Now by faith, I do not solely mean a spiritual or religious faith. While I am a man of faith and personally believe that having a higher power in your life helps you stay focused and grounded, I do not force my beliefs on anyone. They work for me and how I choose to live my life. My faith directs my daily ethical thoughts and actions, and I've witnessed this pattern in others as well. As life progresses and we encounter tough situations, having a deeply rooted faith helps us to navigate those moments with a higher level of grace and ease.

Faith can and should also be approached from a faith-in-self standpoint. Evaluating your faith in this way means measuring whether or not you have faith in your abilities to pursue and accomplish the goals you choose. Many people have goals that stretch beyond their personal faith in themselves, which creates an immediate identity gap and an emotional separation from confidence. So, the first step for you now is to choose a number that correlates with your perceived level of faith in your life—either from a spiritual perspective, a faith-in-self perspective, or you can take the average of both. I always recommend erring on the side of an egoless, honest, lower number so you give yourself ample space to shift and upgrade in that area in the next phase. If you protect your ego and go too high, you'll leave little room and motivation to focus on upgrading that area of your life when it may actually be a necessary root to focus on.

Family

The next root is family. In evaluating this area, your goal is to take an honest look at the relationships you have with your family. You can choose to look at your immediate family or include your extended family too. This is best measured by thinking about how well connected your family is to you and how confident you are in your family's support if and when you may need them. Do you feel you share a deep bond with your immediate family? Do you have their support? If you needed something, would your family drop everything to help you? Would you do the same for them? This same measurement can be directed towards your extended family. Are they present when you need them? Are you connected to them in a deeper way than simply chatting at holidays and the occasional family reunion?

I personally find this area to be so important because I need this root to function mentally. If my family root isn't deep, I can't give speeches, post on social media, write books, etc. It's the base of me that keeps me sound of heart to serve. As with the faith root, you can also choose to assign different numbers for your immediate and extended families, or you can choose to average the two and select that number for the depth of this root in your life.

Friends

Now you have the **friends** root. This is the family you choose. When life goes awry, we need to have great friends and colleagues to lean on. The connection we share with our friends and the investment they have in our lives is vastly different than our connections we have with family. For one, we often spend more time with these people than we do with our extended family. We need to have this solid base in life when we run into trying times. This area can sometimes be measured by reflecting on a single question. If you needed someone to drive an hour to your home at three o'clock in the morning to help you with something, no questions asked, do you have people in your life that would scramble out of bed and chance getting a ticket to speed to your aid? Now, obviously, that's not the gold standard to measure your friendship, nor should it be, but the answer can be very telling of the depth of friendship(s) you have in life. Number this between 0, meaning no friends or poor friendships, and 10, meaning you have so many deep friendships that you cannot add more friends or deepen the friendships you currently have.

Health

Now we have the infamous **health** root. I have always loved the statement, "If you have your health, you have a million dreams. If you do not, you have but one. To be healthy." When you aren't healthy, you cannot focus on the bigger-picture dreams in your heart ,whether it's an actual serious illness that, like my adoptive mom's MS, robs you of the ability to physically accomplish

145

goals—essentially robbing the world of the gift of you—or a less serious but less-than-optimal level of health that forces you to be tired early and often, have headaches, have diminished ability to mentally focus for long periods of time, or any other health issue that slows your progress. Simply being out of shape will keep you out of the winner's circle. Being in shape does something to you physically and mentally that turns average executors into savages when it comes to taking action on their plans and dreams. So, for this area, it's simple: on a scale of 0 – 10, 10 being the best shape of your life and 0 being the worst, where do you stand?

Emotions

Now we come to the final root: **emotions**. When I say emotions, I mean your emotional control in heightened situations. As you know, our emotions lead to actions that we cannot take back— verbal and physical attacks, weak or powerful actions, and even consistent or inconsistent habits. Life is what happens between your plans, and those moments are riddled with unexpected situations—situations that give rise to emotions that trigger unplanned actions that affect the next moments of our lives in ways our logical brain doesn't register until the moment has passed and we have calmed down.

I say this because I've always noticed that when emotions are high, intelligence is low. Science actually shows that an elevated heart rate decreases our ability to properly process our thoughts, and we make more mistakes when we are in heightened state or one of physical or emotional distress than we do when we are in a calmer state. This is why we say things in fights that we don't really mean, like, "I hate you and I wish you would die." This is why we take illogical actions when we're incredibly excited that we wish we could take back, like excitedly attempting to jump off a tree into a lake because everyone is cheering us on, and we fail to clear the shallow end, resulting in two broken legs. Or when you're so happy that you buy the bar a round of beers even though you have barely enough money to pay rent.

When we can't control our emotions in defining moments of life, we end up doing more harm than good for our future. However, when we can control our emotions by knowing how to stay calm, process our thoughts, and make logical choices, we end up setting ourselves up for greatness far more often than we know. So, as you measure this root in your, life simply ask yourself, "How well do I control my emotions in life?" The answer you give will determine the amount of focus you direct towards improving this incredibly important area of your life.

FRUITS

The next step in this process is to look up at the fruits in your life. Fruits are the "fun" parts that we get to see—the areas of our life that come from the work put in to achieve our dreams. What I've noticed is that if we lack in one of our roots, it diminishes our ability to focus and execute on the work needed to produce great fruit. They're connected, as you'll see, and the deeper the roots, the more abundant the fruits. So, if you find yourself falling short in the following areas of fruits, your focus should turn to your roots, and from there, you should determine what must be done to deepen them.

The fruits of your life are simple, but they hold the gold of life that gives you goosebumps. The fruits in your life grow on the branches of your career, finances, education, escape, and L.I.F.T. Each of these branches can grow bigger and more abundant fruit through a focus on the areas of the tree that affect them directly and indirectly, such as the roots, the soil, the sunny environment, and the nutrients given.

Career

Let's start with your **career**. As we practiced with the roots, this branch of your life can be measured by determining, from 0 – 10, how abundant it is with fruits. Take a good look at the career you have now. This is such an incredibly important area in our lives because people literally spend upwards of 50 years in the same profession before retiring at an old age and trying to eke out a few more joys in life. If you hate this area of your life, then it's not only "not exciting"; it's draining. If you love this area of your life, then life is not just livable; it's exciting and fulfilling.

In determining how abundant this branch is with fruit, sit back and ask yourself, "Does the thought of doing this career until I retire bring me a positive or negative feeling?" If you find it brings you a negative feeling, then you have to decide how negative: 0 being you hate it, and 5 being you dislike it but it's not killing you inside. If you find it brings you a positive feeling, then you have to determine how positive: 6 being you don't dislike it but you're OK going to work every day and find some joy in what you do, and 10 being you have found the career you were put on this planet to do. My personal hope is that everyone on this planet shoots for, and someday experiences, their 10.

Finances

Next is the area of your **finances**. This area shouldn't take much explanation. Simply assess whether or not you are happy with the amount of money you have to live the life you desire. If you're completely broke, then it would be an obvious 0. A 10 would mean you have more money than you personally know what to do with. This is not a moment to start adopting the world scale and assessing how much money is enough money compared to someone else's dreams. It's a chance for you to measure how much money you personally need to be happy and feel like you've arrived at an income level that makes you almost lose sight of how much you have coming in because you are in your level of abundance.

Education

Education is an interesting aspect to measure because it's not what most people think it is. When you measure the amount of fruit you have on this branch, it should not be tied to schooling education, although you can factor that in. This should be measured in regard to how much you are learning from your life as you live it. Far too many people live an ignorance-is-bliss existence. This short-sighted bliss feels OK because they're blissfully unaware of the greatness they have access to, which would tower over the empty bliss they currently have.

I find that our greatest educator is life and the proactive seeking of knowledge. Knowledge brings awareness, and awareness precedes actions that usher us into beautiful new levels of life. The worst thing I see is individuals who have lived long lives full of rich experiences who have extracted nothing more than a picture on their phone. Life is a powerful teacher if you choose to pay attention in class. It's within life's moments that we can find a wealth of education. It's the proactive seeking of knowledge and understanding from our day-to-day lives that creates the wisdom many desire.

This is why we often meet people who, despite having fewer years spent on this planet, have a greater wealth of wisdom and knowledge. They just started paying greater attention to the education within life earlier than most. Their years produced more wisdom than the years of others. This is why we tell these people they're wise beyond their years.

In this area of your life, you need to be brutally honest about whether or not you have been taking education from life. o would mean you have floated through your life, paying almost no attention to anything around you and gaining no wisdom. 10 would mean you have an excellent practice of consistently looking at your life in a way that extracts wisdom from every moment. Properly measuring this area of your life will lead you to opening your mind to the actions necessary to expand the years within your years.

Escape

Next, we have escape. By this I mean escaping the monotonous day to day and exploring the big blue marble we float through space on and take in all the beauty it has to show us. Many people, unfortunately, live to work instead of working to live. We are the only species on this planet that has to pay to survive on it. We have to work and earn a living to eat and keep a roof over our heads; however, we do not have to live a life of quiet desperation where the closest we get to a dreamy tropical vacation is a magazine clipping we have pinned on our cubicle wall or our dust-covered vision board.

It has never been as easy, throughout all of human history, to access the world around you as it is right this moment. With a passport and a couple clicks of a mouse you can literally be booked on a flight that will take you to the other side of the planet in a matter of hours. You can experience other ways of living. Other foods. Other ecosystems. You can have experiences that will take your breath away and lift your heart to the heavens. Simply hiking a mountain and reaching a peak that casts your eyes on a landscape that puts the Earth in slow motion can wrap you in boundless joy.

When you measure this area of your life, I want you to make a simple delineation: 0 is if you haven't seen anything more than the place you grew up in; 10 is only used if you have seen every inch of this amazing planet we call home. Find your personal number for where you sit between those two. I want that number to sit as a stark reminder of how much life you have left to live and experience.

L.I.F.T.

Finally, we come to the area that I find holds my heart hostage. Your L.I.F.T. This is an acronym that means "life inside for triumph." Simply put, this is your clear purpose and why you live your life the way you do. What gives you motivation to not simply "try" but to "triumph" and succeed? When I meet people, I tend to ask them what lifts their hearts up and keeps them pushing past the hard parts to succeed at a higher level; what their reasoning is for staying the course.

Think of it kind of like a hot air balloon. When you want to elevate the altitude of the balloon, you turn on the fire that heats the air and makes it rise. Your L.I.F.T. is the fire inside your "belly" that, much like the hot air balloon, will allow you to raise your altitude in life. When you measure this area in your life, the goal is to check in internally and determine if you are getting up every day and living your passionate purpose. o would mean that you have no idea at all what it is and, therefore, you're clearly not living it. A 5 would mean you have an idea of what it is, but you're not living it the way you know you should. A 10 would mean you know why you were placed on this planet and you are living out that purpose daily; that you're doing what you love and people love that you are doing it.

Now that you have concrete numbers for your roots and fruits in life, you move on to the shift stage. You can now see the areas holding you back in your life from creating great fruits of your labor and start to create a greater vision—whether it's focusing more on the fruit branches and tending to that area of the tree, or digging into the soil of your life to change your environment, or simply deepening the roots to give your tree the ability to create great fruit.

As conceptual as this may come across at face value, I promise you this carries as much real-life weight as anything you can do. I experienced this firsthand when I went down the path of making my shift. While I have shared some anecdotes about what my life looked like after working on my roots and fruits, I didn't share the catalyst of that journey. I remember waking up on day on New Year's Day and rolling off the right side of my bed to my feet. My brain seemed to slosh around like a bowl of punch from the previous night's intake of alcohol. I could faintly hear the breathing of the woman sleeping behind me who'd made it home to my bed. I made the long three-foot trek to the bathroom, flipped the switch, and as I crossed the threshold by stepping both of my bare feet onto the freezing cold floor, I closed the door behind me.

Almost like a scene out of a movie I felt my stomach twist a little as my head simultaneously started aching a bit. I'm not sure if it was the light trying to poke its way past my slightly open eyelids, standing up too fast, or the baby hangover I was experiencing, but I pushed my hands down onto the sink's edge and propped myself up so as not to fall down from the stars I started seeing. With my head sunken down and forwards, feeling like a bowling ball hanging off my body, I slowly lifted it up to take a look in the mirror. As my eyes opened and I took in the sight of myself, I felt something.

I would describe this feeling as a wave, but not the kind you see at a beach on a sunny day, the kind that flows through your body and crashes into your soul. This wave was of shame. My tree was in horrible soil, being deprived of the essential nutrients it needed to deepen or supply the roots with what they needed. So, obviously, the fruits were also in lack and therefore not present in any health of abundance. This was the moment I realized I didn't like this man looking back at me. I would never want my daughter to be with a man like me, would never want my sons to be like me, my mom would never have approved of this life, and my God wouldn't let me into heaven like this. Something had to change.

This was the moment when I made the conscious decision to put my energy towards my roots and fruits to shift my identity and change my life. I went to work on all the roots first. I removed myself from the friend groups and environments that didn't serve where I wanted to be in the future. I focused on my faith first by repenting and asking my God for forgiveness as I spent more time in scripture and church. I started getting back in touch with my family and friends and deepening those relationships again. I got back into exercising almost daily so I could feel great in my skin again. Then I got in touch with the emotional side of myself and addressed all the hard feelings that had arisen for me along this journey of asking for and giving forgiveness. It was the actual work necessary to deepen and strengthen the root system in my life.

To my joy the world accepted me in all my disarray. I found pride again in my faith and telling people I was a Christian. My friends and family were proud to claim me and wanted me around more often than before, when I was honestly not of character. I got into a shape that I was proud to show off on hot days on the boat because I had spent time working on my mind and body during those hard workout sessions. Most of all, I emotionally fell back in love internally with a guy that I previously didn't like and wasn't fond of spending time alone with. Me. I learned to manage my self-hate and turn it around, as well as manage heated emotional moments far better than I had in recent history. I had tended to my roots, and it was showing up in my life amazingly. In fact, it started to show up in my fruits as well.

I wasn't a person who enjoyed reading or educating myself at that time and although I heard constantly how important it was, I never invested into my education after college. Once I started trying to learn on purpose, I realized how much of life I wasn't actually learning from, even though there were amazing lessons right in front of my eyes, and I started to yearn for more. This led to me seeking a new level of joy inside of my career. I was previously going through the motions without true vigor and drive to show up and serve the world through my work. I was doing, but I wasn't really doing it. Once I did, I found myself far more impactful and far more fulfilled. Which led to me making more money. I was increasing my income in ways that felt good and left me feeling worthy of it. I was also smarter with my purchases and saved more often than I ever had before.

This led me to have more freedom and income to actually take more trips and explore the world. I traveled and saw more sights, met great people, developed even deeper relationships, and learned more about life than I knew there was to know at the time. It was around this time that I was gifted with something I pray everyone receives. The gift of knowing why you're here. The reason you were placed on this planet. Whether right or wrong, my life seemed to click into the place I still happen to be—sharing all the craziness of life I've experienced through my speaking, coaching, and writing to teach lessons and bring joy to those still struggling. I've never felt a deeper connection to purpose and passion than I do now. I believe that is what led to my wife and my life coming back into reach. I had shifted my identity through the actions of focusing on my roots and fruits to become the person capable and worthy of having the things I now have in my life. Something quite literally and person can do.

The roots and fruits you just completed is one of a collection of exercises we at Identity Shift Coaching work people through in the See Phase of the Shift Method Coaching Suite. If you'd like to complete another exercise, I recommend you head to www.SlowOrGo.co and take the Slow or Go Identity Quiz. In the See Phase, another area that will help you prepare for the Shift Phase is determining what type of identity you currently have operating in the background, which the Slow Or Go Quiz determines. This personal operation determines how you approach opportunity and opposition in life, which affects your life without you consciously noticing it. It shows you where your life-hindering fear lives. We all have goals that are slowed and stalled by fear. If we didn't have fear, then that thing would already be done by now. This quiz helps you uncover how you're operating, what your fears are, how it's affected your life, and what you need to do to shift into the ideal identity capable of achieving your dreams.

REFLECTION SECTION

Deep Shift – What is your deepest root and why?

Short Shift – What is your shortest root and why?

Abundant Shift – Which is your most abundant fruit branch and why?

Empty Shift – Which branch has the least fruit and why?

CHAPTER 7

THE SHIFT METHOD: SHIFT

Ninety-two percent of people, when polled in a University of Scranton study, reported that they did not accomplish the goals they set for themselves each year. I spend my waking hours actively working with and studying high-aspiring humans with verbalized goals repeatedly leaving their lips. At this point in my career, I have a system and a dedication to my clients' success that places them in the top 8 percent of achievement-seeking humans around 90 percent of the time. I am always uncovering new areas of issue for people that I had never previously encountered. It's mind boggling how many reasons exist to thwart a person's progress in the direction of their dreams.

When I first became a coach, I didn't know what the issue was when it came to people not accomplishing goals. Even though I had people tell me with vigor and passion how dedicated they were, it seemed like they would shut down at the first sight of hard work. When I say hard work, I mean work that was hard relative to their level of hard. They'd do what they deemed hard and then shut down with frustration and/or anger-ridden excuses. They would never grasp the concept that the level of hard work their dreams demanded of them would almost always lie outside of the desired level of hard work they wanted to give. Logically, however, if it wasn't harder, then they would already have the thing they wanted most.

If you consider the fact that the things they had attained felt comfortable to have and achieve, then it would stand to reason that the moment they could put in the hard work well above the level they currently have, then the desired future goal(s) would feel just as easy and comfortable as the levels they currently have. Meaning if you are used to doing harder work than what's needed to achieve your goal, then success would, in fact, feel easy. The fact that your level of hard work isn't that high should clarify why it's going to feel harder to reach that next level. This is what people talk about when they mention expanding your comfort zone.

So how do you do that? How do you make the hard work to achieve your goal feel easy?

What does this have to do with the Shift Phase?

Everything.

SUFFERING & SUCCESS

The 15-year-old me, who had the desired to achieve the goal of being successful at the high school level in the sport of football, the 18-year-old me, who desired to be successful at the college level, and the 22-year-old me, who desired being successful at the NFL level had to increase the level of what I deemed hard work. That next level was always a far cry from what was comfortable in that moment. In order to shift into that identity at each level, I had to work, meaning I had to take actions repeatedly above any level of comfort I had. Daily. Actions end suffering. When you are suffering the pain of not achieving a goal after an outpouring of effort, the answer isn't to stop taking actions. It's to take bigger, bolder, and scarier actions. It's those actions and only those actions that end suffering.

Take Columbia's Oscar Mosquera, an Olympic weightlifter. Oscar is the kind of passion-driven human I love to hear about. He yearned to one day win a gold medal and be the world's greatest. A feat that is by no means easy in any chosen venture. He trained for years just to be able to compete in the Olympics, and in 2004, he earned his first opportunity. To his dismay, he finished fifth and did not receive a medal. The length of a journey to this level in the world alone is enough to burn a person out. On top of that to not achieve your goal creates a level of suffering even fewer can endure. Oscar was still suffering inside because he knew what he wanted to achieve and that he had not yet done it.

He had a choice: give up on the dream and endure that suffering for the rest of his life or spend the next four years taking even more action and working even harder to accomplish his goal of a gold medal. Oscar chose the latter. Fast forward four years of suffering silently and working past the pain to achieve his goal, and he shows up to the Beijing Olympics in 2008 ready to go after his dream again. Unfortunately, he wouldn't even place because he was unable to record a lift in competition due to an injury that later resulted in surgery. For 99 percent of people this would equate to a level of physical and emotional suffering necessary to shut someone's dream down forever. Not Oscar.

Not only did he compete again four years later and fall short of his goal again by taking second place, he continued even further beyond that for another four years. It was the 2012 Olympics in Brazil that would culminate in a gold medal for Oscar after 16 years of suffering with the pain of not accomplishing his goal. When he finally won the medal, his heart sought for so long, all he could do was take his shoes off and place them in front of the bar, kneel, and cry. Imagine the level of action it took day in and day out to end that suffering. It did not happen because he wanted it badly and had done enough hard work to deserve it. It happened because he went vastly beyond his comfort zone and took actions at the level his dream required.

That is the human spirit at its finest, and it's a testament to the level of effort your dreams will demand of you. If you aren't willing to go to that level for your dream, then you have no other choice than to accept the pain and suffering that comes along with it. You either get suffering or success, and the determinant is the action you take to shift.

Again, it's the actions that lead to a shift in your identity. When 15-year-old me, who wanted to create a stronger body, inadvertently created a stronger self simultaneously, it happened ONLY through action. Not desire. It's not enough to know what actions you need to take, like the ones you've uncovered in the See Phase of the Shift Method. You need to actually take the actions outlined for your life in order to make an identity shift. There are too many people who put in the effort of getting clarity on the work they must do, only to sit on their butts and feel an odd sense of undeserved accomplishment. Then they don't put forth the effort to execute on those actions they know they need to take. So, you know what to work on? Great. NOW GO DO IT. If not, you'll continue to experience the suffering of not having what you want most because you'll never take the actions to make the shift.

THE WEIGHTS OF LIFE

Now on to making the hard work easy. Sound almost too good to be true? Spoiler alert—it is. See, most people want to achieve their dreams without experiencing any pain on the path. People want it to be enough to just want it enough. They want the hard things by doing what is easy. Life doesn't work that way. When you set out to do things the easy way in life, success will always feel hard, mostly because the level of hard work needed to achieve that lofty goal will continue to sit outside their perceived level of their max effort. It's only when they lean in and start attacking the hard things in life that their capabilities and strength will surpass the level of hard work necessary to achieve their goals. Then that level of hard work becomes easy.

This is the exact reason why the successful people you look up to make their success look easy. It is easy to them. The work is not different; it's the exact same work. However, when you approach that level of work, it's hard, draining, and takes you all week to get it done. Whereas they step up to the plate on Monday, knock it out by noon, and are on to the next task, leaving you wide eyed and amazed. Your brain explodes at the sheer mention of the next thing they're working on after what they just got done doing. It's simply a strength issue. Mental, emotional, and at times physical.

At one point, they were just as weak and were struggling as much as you are. They just took the actions to shift and, over time, built up to a level where their perceived level of hard work was so high that anything underneath that level felt easy.

Imagine you enter a weight room and go over to the dumbbell rack. You try to lift a 50lb dumbbell, and it feels like it's glued to the rack, no matter how hard you pull. So you walk away and just assume that it's impossible for anyone to lift that weight. To your astonishment, someone else walks over, grabs the weight off the rack, and starts throwing it around like a feather. What just happened?

Well, it's plain and simple. That person is stronger than you. The weight that you can't seem to pick up is a weight they warm up with before moving on to weights you didn't realize any human could lift. It's a physical representation of what's happening in your life when you try to reach a higher level. Regardless of the level you have already achieved, there is always another level for you.

That person, at some point, was definitely weaker and scrawnier than you are at this moment; they just built up the strength over time, so the weight that was hard for them to move eventually became easy to lift. They chose the hard but necessary way to make that weight easy. They could have never lifted that heavy and hard weight if they worked out with lighter and easier weights every day. They chose the weights that were heavy to them at the time and built up the strength with those level by level. They had to continuously push their current level of hard and heavy so they would eventually have the strength to lift that weight.

Once they were in motion, they just kept lifting the weight until it was easy and fun to lift weights, and all the heavy weights became easier and lighter in time. That's why strong and successful people look like they're having fun. They are. They enjoy lifting the weights of life every day. They enjoy getting and staying strong. Their success isn't a chore; it's a blessing.

The only difference is that in life the weights you have to lift aren't as visible as the weights in a weight room. Hard often sneaks up on you. While you can walk into a weight room and see the weights on a rack, in life, those weights show up in work, relationships, business, and your health in ways you never saw coming. It's when your business demands you to juggle multiple tasks to stay afloat in hard times. It's when you need to develop habits in your relationship that feel like you're dragging a boulder up an asphalt hill. It's any time you are confronted with a set of habits or big actions that feel like the hardest thing in the world to take on.

THE H.A.R.D. WAY

This is life giving you the hard work necessary to achieve your goal that you're tasked with making easy over time. How do you make those hard things easy? It's simple—by doing things the H.A.R.D. way. A friend of mine, who is also a coach, mentioned that I should alleviate the weight of how this exercise sounds by calling it the easy way, but to be honest, this book isn't for people who are drawn to wanting things the easy way in life. This book is for people committed to the idea of earning their identity; people who want to be at a level where they have pride in their strength, which only comes from doing the hard work necessary to make their lives feel easy and fun.

The H.A.R.D. Method is a simple and effective strategy to help you start making your identity shift. While there are many other exercises within the Shift Method coaching programs, this is one of my favorite tools to guide the actions you can take to make a shift using the insights you garnered from the Roots and Fruits exercise. To get your H.A.R.D. Method worksheet, head to www. IdentityShiftBook.com/resources.

H.A.R.D. stands for habits, actions, reactions, and drivers. When you inform this framework with the insights from the SEE stage, you will come out with a set of habits, actions, reactions, and drivers that will be hard to consistently execute. They will be the heavy weights of life you choose to lift to build your strength. If you can stay in the weight room of life and do this hard work, you will make life, and your next levels of success, feel easy and enjoyable to lift.

Habits

So let's start with **habits**. With the H.A.R.D. Method, the goal is to take a look at all the areas in your roots and fruits and determine which habits you must have running in your life to increase the depth of a root, or the fruit on a branch, by one. Not habits to take your number to a 10 but to increase it by a value of 1. Not only do these habits help you make progress over time; they are also paramount in upgrading your identity. You are what you repeatedly do, and habits are the path to that person.

This means every day you should focus on activating habits to increase your faith in a higher power or yourself. Maybe you'll read a religious text or say affirmations to yourself every morning. For your family, you can infuse habits of family dinners or, at minimum, weekly solo time with each member of your immediate family. For extended family, maybe you call one new person to catch up each week and solidify those relationships.

For friends you may take time to set up special monthly outings to create bonding experiences and deepen your connections. You may also expand your friend groups to people who can aid you in reaching your next level, while possibly removing friends who are keeping you small.

Health may be as simple as walking outside instead of sitting down for lunch each day or choosing to tackle your first triathlon by adding a mile a week to your running regimen instead of just going to the gym each day with no plan.

When it comes to your emotional control, you may actively place yourself in an uncomfortable situation each week to slowly develop the habits of responding to difficult situations in a calmer manner. This could be joining Toastmasters to learn how to speak.

Or joining a coed sports league, or even chess league, to put yourself in heated emotional situations that come from competition.

For your career, you may find yourself starting a habit of meeting with people each month who have careers you look at with a certain level of interest so you can start developing habits of consistently researching things that pique your interest.

For education you could start a daily journaling practice where you recap each day and extract three lessons learned. This develops a habit of consciously seeing what's happening in your life, and the implications, without letting them slide by unnoticed anymore.

In your finances area you could develop the habit of saving a percentage of money each month for one big trip you'll take at the end of each year. This means you'd have to make sacrifices every single month for a big payoff at the end of the year. So, the next time your friends ask to go out for drinks, you may have to hold the habit of saying no, putting the money aside, and not touching it at all.

In your escape area, you could actually choose to piggyback on the finance habits you've engrained. You could develop a monthly habit of researching new destinations you'd like to travel to and start planning the trip you'll take at the end of the year with the money saved.

For your L.I.F.T. you can develop a habit of trying something new that sparks your interest each month—something that allows you to chase your passion, even if it only makes sense to your heart and not to you or anyone in your life. Maybe you've heard about a hobby that sounds fun and interesting. Maybe there's a community of people you want to serve and help. Build a habit of trying new things in life, and you'll find that even though it's hard, it will pay off in the long run.

Actions

Next, we need to address the **actions** piece of the H.A.R.D. Method. While habits are ongoing and require consistent commitment, actions are the big bangs that can provide immediate benefits. They're usually just scary to attempt because of the risk/reward factors. Life is riddled with these big moments, which I like to call defining moments. These are the moments where big actions happen, and they quickly move the needle forward or backward. These moments can begin a set of habits, or they can take place once a habit has set you up to capitalize on the big action. You are going to have to choose the actions that you know will move the needle, and you'll know they're the right actions because they'll make you freeze in fear at the initial thought of them.

If you need to take big actions for your spiritual faith, you may choose to commit your life to that higher power. Or maybe you choose to follow a different religion altogether. These are just simple examples, and only you know which big actions you need to take. If it's a faith in self that needs to be established, you may have to take an action that allows you to build that self-worth through finding success past a fear. If it's a fear of public speaking, then get on a stage. If it's a fear of going on a date, then go ask someone out to dinner. The action has to be risky enough where you'll feel funky if you fail because that is a sure-fire way to know that you'll jump for joy when you succeed, and it will fill you with pride and faith in yourself.

When it comes to family and friends, you usually have to take an action that is far outside your comfort zone. It always seems to be that way with family, whether it's immediate or extended family, or close friends. Due to family and friends being all about relationships, and relationships being hard to manage, the actions in this area tend to be in the realm of apologies or appreciation. Both happen to be weirdly difficult to do. You do end up putting yourself in a situation where the other person may not respond the way you want, but you have to take the action. These are actions that may backfire but have the potential to create deeper relationships.

With health the big action is likely doing something drastic that scares you. Maybe you publicly commit to working out every day. Or you choose to throw all the food in your pantry away and start from scratch with only healthy food. Maybe you take the action of joining a new workout facility or you hire a trainer. It all will boil down to doing something you don't want to do but you know will help you be healthier in your life.

For big actions in the emotional sphere, this is typically planning to put yourself in a situation you know will spike your emotions, knowing you'll have to navigate those waters. This could be openly making an apology that someone may not accept or know how to handle from you. This might even be doing a random act of kindness for someone that will put you in a position to accept gratitude if this is something you're not comfortable with.

For the career area, there are typically two types of big actions that move the needle and are scary enough to make you feel amazing if you succeed. The first is quitting your job to take on another riskier but bigger-opportunity career. The second is starting a business and putting yourself out into the world to "kill what you eat." There are obviously many more areas where you can take big actions in your career that scare you and put you in a position to have a high risk and high return.

For finances, the big action you take may be an investment. Typically, when we're talking about high risk and high return, it is a financial discussion. Now, I do not want you to read this book and go off and make a high-risk financial decision because that would obviously be unwise. Take your time and find a calculated risk option with professional financial advisors. You could also take the risky action of betting on yourself to do something that could return money. Maybe create a piece of art or new business venture that could be a risk of your time, and possibly money, but return as increased income.

For education, you could take a big action of enrolling in a higher education program or venture into a coaching program or master-mind to grow your knowledge. You could also choose to reach out to a hero of yours and see if you could get a few moments of their time to answer a few of your pressing questions. Education at a level high enough to change your life is not easy to come by, and the actions you must take to attain that knowledge should be scary.

In my opinion, the big actions you can take in your escape area of life should be pretty clear. Get yourself out there and take a big action of booking a trip to explore the world. Cash in your vacation days. Clear your client schedule. Pay for the flight and hotel. Just put it in your calendar and go. Far too many people miss out on life's greatest experiences because they're too scared to just book a trip and go. Also, you don't have to travel around the world to explore something new. I'm pretty sure there are beautiful areas nearby your home that have yet to be graced by your presence. Go find those and actually schedule a time to visit them.

When it comes to your L.I.F.T. big actions, I recommend taking an action of pursuing a passion. If I were to pry deep enough, I'm sure I would uncover a hidden part of your heart that is passion-ate about something you haven't let see the light of day. The big action you can and should take in this area of your life is to own and pursue something that brings you closer to your purpose by chasing your life's passions. It's these paths of passion that lead you down a road where you stumble into the pothole of your purpose—the thing that L.I.F.T.s your heart and elevates your life.

Reactions

The final two sections of the H.A.R.D. Method, reactions and drivers, are less detailed; however, I believe they may be the most important aspects of the method as well as the hardest to master—pun intended. The first we'll discuss is **reactions**. When I think about reactions, I'm considering all of the unexpected moments that happen across our life paths leaving us with little to no time to make incredibly hard choices that all have repercussions. Choices that are difficult to make and usually irreversible.

The worst part is that we're usually aware in the moment of how these choices can be detrimental to our futures. The biggest problem I believe we face isn't the unexpected moment, however. These unexpected moments are going to happen because that's how life works, and these moments can actually bring great opportunity to our lives. Winning the lottery or getting an unexpected promotion are examples of these types of moments; they are obviously not always negative simply because they were unexpected. I actually believe the greatest detriment we face is in fact arriving at these moments without any plans whatsoever to master them.

When pitchers throw a batter a curveball in a game, they've typically practiced and planned in advance how to swing at that pitch. So, when they get a curveball, they know how to make adjustments to still have a chance at hitting a home run. When life throws you a curveball, you need to have practiced and planned as well. A plan allows you to calm your nerves in unexpected moments and make a calculated decision to give yourself a chance to hit a home run. When you have a plan in place, you actually step up to the plate a little more often, and with more confidence, because you know how you'll approach unexpected curveballs.

So the goal is simple when it comes to reactions. Consider what you would do, how you would react, if something unexpected were to take place. This does not mean that you let your brain trail off into distant fear-filled tangents. Instead, think logically about what may happen and how you may handle that situation. If you ask for a raise and your boss says no, how will you react? How will you react if he or she says yes? If you get onto a sales call and the person says yes or no, how will you react? If you go into a sporting event, how will you remember to keep your cool if a call doesn't go your way? How would you think through a difficult conversation if you child came to you with something you didn't expect?

When you think about this stage of the H.A.R.D. Method, I don't want you to stress about coming up with the perfect reaction to any or all situations. One, because you cannot ever come to know what situations you will encounter in life and therefore cannot plan perfectly. Two, because the goal is not to actually have a perfect planned reaction to every moment. The goal is to know how to approach any unexpected situation by applying a patterned thought process. This thought process is actually the tool you're trying to master. It's the process that holds the magic, not the definitive, silver-bullet answer you need to have prepared in the moment for every specific situation you encounter.

This is one of the most critical aspects of the H.A.R.D. Method because it's the reactions in these moments that allow you to be able to start and/or stay on track with the habits and actions you're taking. The worst thing I find that happens when people start taking big actions or launching their habits is that a singular event can derail everything before they get started or quickly after they begin. This happens whenever you enter into a new stage of life and you do not have a plan, or process for quick planning, to navigate defining moments as they come to pass. The simplest process I can share is one that accidentally came out in a coaching session with my clients. I find that I have many interesting operating principles that I do so autonomously that I rarely even notice them. I'm triggered, I begin a habit, it runs its course, and I'm oblivious to what happened. At this point, they're genuine automatic reactions. One happens to be the way I handle all unexpected moments, good or bad.

I call this reaction process my seven-second ritual. It's provided me so much benefit over the years that I genuinely swear by it now that I've noticed it. One of my clients asked me how I would handle a situation they had experienced with their staff in a meeting in which they were presenting the next year's goals and where the team fit into the big picture. One staff member, who was apparently slightly disgruntled, stated, "So we're setting goal we probably won't achieve just like this year?" Having that statement be fired off in your direction in a meeting that was previously positive would leave anyone in a spiked emotional state, whether it be an emotion of anger, frustration, or shame. It's hard to handle a situation like that, but it must be handled properly in an instant. I rattled off the exact process I use and that I'm about to share with you now.

First, I close my mouth and literally commit to saying nothing. Again, when emotions are high, intelligence is low, and I do not want something to come out that's born of unintelligent emotion that I may not be able to retract. Next, at that moment, I take a big breath in and start counting to seven in my head. The breath is exhaled by the end of the seven count, and I've taken that time to let the emotion of joy, anger, etc., settle in. I let myself be pissed or happy for those moments, and then I trigger a decision. The decision is a definitive choice I will make regarding how to proceed.

The brain is a powerful computer that quite literally has a mind of its own. However, I need that mind to be mine so that I can harness its power. When you point the brain in a direction, it will use all of its power to find the things you send it looking for, like a dog with a scent that's sent off to find something. The two things the brain typically goes looking for in these moments are excuses or solutions. Most people let the brain head down the path of least resistance—and also least abundance. Excuses. There are always going to be a multitude of excuses, and they're easy to find, not to mention, they have the potential to let us off the hook with ease. I hate the path of least resistance because it's usually the path of least success and, as you already know, the easy way makes life hard.

The brain doesn't always have a natural trigger to go looking for solutions, but that's where success is found. For example, if I asked you to take me to the airport at 5:00 a.m., you'd immediately start down a path of every reason why you would not be able to. Whereas you could have just as equally went looking for reasons that you could drive me. It's just a natural trigger at this point. So, in those seven seconds, you have a moment to collect yourself and make a choice when you arrive at the eighth second. As mentioned before, wherever you set the direction of your brain, it will find a way.

I'm sure you've realized that I am a solutions human. I don't like excuses because excuses, good or bad, get in the way of my goals. The moment an excuse gets in the way, I realize that I let the excuse become bigger than my dream. You'll never have success if you allow excuses to become bigger than your dream, no matter how viable and genuine the excuses. I have kids but I don't let raising them become an excuse to kill my goals; I find solutions to become a great dad and achieve my dreams.

Once you have arrived at that eighth second, and you've made the decision to find a solution, sit down and/or stop yourself. Unless it's an emergency, obviously. Once stopped, the next step is to process your plan for response based upon one thought. *What will make the next moments of my life great?* The choice you make right now to take action on will determine the quality of the next moments of your life. In these moments, you need to lean towards the action that improves your next moments, even if every part of your soul doesn't want to do that thing.

Knowing what's right and doing what's right are two completely different things. Most people know what's right and do what's wrong, so they negatively affect the next moments of their life. They do this because they don't have emotional control and they have no process to manage unexpected high-intensity moments. So they begin a downhill slide that becomes borderline impossible to recover from. This is what throws people off track for the short, and eventually long, term.

Once you've made the choice of the proper action, you need to take that specific action. This may mean an apology you do not want to make but you know is deserved. This happens for me as a parent when my kids point out something I did wrong, and as "Dad," I hate that I have to admit fault and apologize. This action may also look like harnessing your anger and desire to retort to someone who's being rude or disrespectful. On the flip side, you may also need to muster the confidence to do or say something that is outside your comfort zone but necessary to make the next moments right. Like the person getting bullied, or being taken advantage of in a situation, you may need to rear up in that moment and say something you've never said before to make the next moments of your life better.

I've had many moments where people say things to me that I would love to use as fuel to explode back on them. I know, however, that I don't want to be in a long, drawn-out fight or go to jail for hitting someone. I also want to be able to stay on track with my plan and goals for that day. So, I choose to bite my tongue, move on, and experience my life in a better place in the very near future because that action is what's needed to make the next moments better. I've also realized that sometimes the best punishment for a disrespectful and spiteful person is for them to continue living their own life as is. So I leave them alone to their misery.

Now you see why I believe that reactions are less in-depth to think through regarding your individual situation, but they stand to possibly be more important in the long run. These moments will occur. If you handle them with a planned set of reactions, you will set yourself up for great success. This is how successful people on a mission seem to just let things roll off their backs like a duck. There just isn't time to engage in low-level energy expenditure that detracts from the main direction. They master moments to move mountains in their life.

Drivers

The final aspect of this method is drivers. Drivers are simple. They're the reasons why you're sticking to each habit, action, and reaction. For each of habit, action, and reaction, you should write out why you commit to executing on that plan. Why will you stay the course when things are easy, and especially when things are hard? What drives your heart to do what must be done in that eighth-second moment, even though you do not want to? What driving force is keeping you from breaking in a difficult habit, even though it's taking longer than desired to solidify it and make it easy? What is driving you to master the unexpected moments, no matter how crazy and complicated they feel?

Your drivers are the root reasons behind the ensuing actions in planning, executing, and consciously adjusting in the moment. That is how you stay the course over time and take the actions to make an identity shift in life. These habits, actions, reactions, and drivers are hard to plug into your life and execute on, but doing them over time becomes an investment that returns an upgraded identity that has elevated your life.

This Shift Phase of the Shift Method has many more steps and exercises, but this exercise alone has the power to change your life if you implement it. You should now have all the insights needed to begin a powerful shift in your life, capable of upgrading how you operate to elevate your existence. You've seen the areas in your blind spots as well as dreams you can expand into for ongoing success in life. You've also now learned how to plan and execute the H.A.R.D. way so life becomes easy. This is how to truly make a shift in your life.

REFLECTION SECTION

Repeat Shift – What habits do you know must be added to your life that are difficult but will increase your strength and capabilities once practiced consistently?

Shift into Action – What are two or three big actions you know must be taken in the next seven to ten days to move the needle forward for your identity?

What shift made sense? – When in your past did you mismanage a reaction? In hindsight, what should you have done differently?

What shift drives you? – What is the greatest "why" in your life that drives you to stay the course and succeed?

CHAPTER 8

THE SHIFT METHOD: SUSTAIN

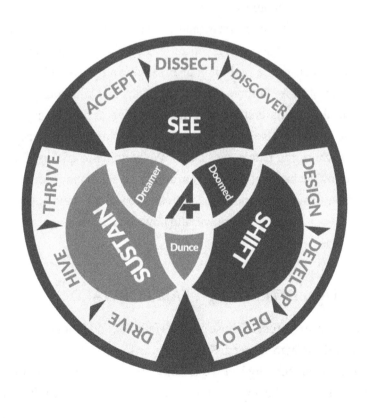

179

How do you win in life? By winning the long game. By sustaining when all others wither away in the face of the difficulties life throws at them. You're going to have setbacks; it's inevitable. It's life. It's those moments that build your strength to endure in the long game of life.

These setbacks can come from internal and external sources. Internally, they come from having a negative self-image and self-talk, not following through with something and feeling shameful, or not being able to muster the energy or passion to commit again. If you allow these internal setbacks to become an anchor, you stay sunk at the bottom of the ocean of your life, unable to rise up and see the beautiful blue skies of your dreams.

Externally, they come from failures that crush your spirit, desire, and any hopes of success. If you allow these to break you, you will walk away from the path of your passions and purpose because the pain of those failures infects your heart and kills your pride.

You already understand how the drive, hive, and thrive aspects of the Sustain Phase operate. How you can bring these aspects to life is where the true power exists. We're going to address both handling the internal and external aspects of sustaining—internal meaning how you respond to failures; external meaning how you check your progress, your hive, and how you pursue higher levels.

SUSTAIN INTERNALLY: FAIL FORWARD

Excuses are the fuel of those who are failures, and failures are the fuel of those who succeed. Failures are an inevitable aspect of life, and they can actually be used for more than an excuse to not try again. In fact, I believe the root of an inability to sustain is fear.

If you weren't afraid of doing something, even in the slightest, then it would already be done by now. Not doing something is usually tied to a fear of failure—a fear that I believe shouldn't exist. I'm not special and I'm not crazy. I'm simply aware of how to reframe failures to use them as fuel and, in fact, fail forward in any area of life.

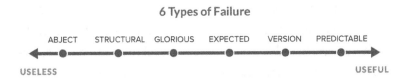

6 Types of Failure

	ABJECT	STRUCTURAL	GLORIOUS	EXPECTED	VERSION	PREDICTABLE

USELESS   USEFUL

I use a process called reframing failures. This process takes a hard look at the fears that hold us back from taking action solely based on the possibility of failing. Unfortunately, we tend to be so afraid of failure that the fear gets bigger than our goals and keeps us stuck. So even if we do get traction, we never sustain the path to create the momentum necessary to succeed and truly make an identity shift. You can grab your Reframing Failure worksheet at www.IdentityShiftBook.com/resources.

The issue we have with failures is not the fact that they occur; the problem is that we don't understand how to capitalize on them in a way that gives us clarity and comfort. If I could give you a process to genuinely use any failure as a powerful fuel for success, would you attempt scarier actions, knowing you might fail? If I could give you a process that could guarantee you find the silver lining in each setback and that any bold action ending in failure would, in fact, inspire you to step back up to the plate again and again, would you use it? While I know there's a percentage of people who would still adamantly say "no," I know there's a percentage of people that would excitedly say "yes." Those "yes" people are my people.

Whether you're one of my people or not, you're about to learn how to reframe failures—something that may swing you to our side if you think you could be in the "no" category. Failure isn't black and white; in fact, there are six distinct levels of failure. By looking at each level individually, we can see the different ways people perceive these situations and we can extract lessons from each level to utilize these failures as fuel to succeed. These levels of failure are, in order or most detrimental to least, abject, structural, glorious, common, version, and predictable.

Abject Failure

Abject failure is a failure that you have no, or perceive no, ability to come back from. It's maximum failure, like death or a complete ending of something with no chances of it starting back up again or being fixed. If someone or something physically dies and there's no reviving it, then you have experienced an abject failure. In these instances, we experience such trauma and pain that we turn our hearts from the memory in hopes of preserving what little joy we have. There's just too much pain to even think about it, so why subject ourselves to that pain? So, we take no lessons from the situation simply because we can't handle the hurt of revisiting it in our head and hearts.

Structural Failure

Structural failure is a failure where a critical aspect of something fails, but it is fixable. It would just take a great deal of energy and effort to repair. A relationship falls apart due to infidelity. An athlete loses a limb in a freak accident. I have seen marriages recover from infidelity. I have also seen athletes return to competition with prosthesis. The problem is that those are the less-than1-percent situations. In fact, most people just give up and move on because a critical component failed and it would be too big of a hill to climb to fix it. It's not the end, but for the vast majority, it becomes the end. So we, again, feel a wall of pain and failure that hurts so bad we tuck tail and run from the memory and never revisit it to extract any lessons to learn. So, we gather no fuel from these failures.

Glorious Failure

Glorious failure is a failure that is so mind blowing and drive deflating that we just sit back, light a cigar, and smoke it while we watch everything burn to the ground. The business fails because the market turns or crashes. My favorite personal trainer, who I've been working with for years, moves out of town so I give up working out and gain weight again. My company merges with another company, and I get fired. We feel helpless to do anything, so yet again, the pain of the failure deters us from spending any emotional energy focusing on what happened. So, we press on with our lives with no more wisdom and no fuel from this failure—only anger, resentment, disdain, and fear to take later action because the thought of this happening again is paralyzing.

These top three areas of failure are, unfortunately, the areas that the vast majority of people live in. Every failure that happens in life is blown out of proportion. We find illogical reasons to make everything seem so much worse than it is. So the pain sits right below the surface, right alongside the constant fear of experiencing anything similar ever again. So when the relationship fails, we tell ourselves we're unlovable and swear off all partners because we don't want to feel that abject or structural failure again. When we lose the job, we tell ourselves we'll never find another job like that ever again, so we don't interview for that job ever again because the fear of rejection would hurt us too badly. Then there's the bottom three, which are the levels I choose to embrace.

Common Failure

Common failure is the failure that created the apology. When you consider what an apology is by definition, it's an acknowledgement of a personal failure. It's a failure all the same, but your acknowledgment of the cause leads you to learn something new that will allow you to prevent a similar situation in the future. The key word in that last statement was "learn." In the top three failure levels, most people experience so much pain and anguish that they fail to learn anything. People turn their backs to life's lessons simply because they can't hold space for the pain to provide them with the path to the lesson. When you apologize, you learn, and you can avoid similar failures in the future. You've now given yourself a small amount of fuel to pursue future actions that have the potential to end similarly, but your new insights diminish those chances.

Version Failure

Version failure might be my absolute favorite level of failure to share. I know that sounds odd, but you already inherently understand this level without realizing it, and you may soon actually see why it brings me joy to fail at this level. When we consider our lives and our identities, this level is the perfect fit for upgrading how we operate. See, many failures occur in life with one common denominator: you. You are the common denominator in your problems, and the moment you absorb that reality, you will find a release from the fear of failure that grabs you every time you get to the emotional ledge of taking an action to change your life.

Version failure is the realization that you tried your absolute best in that moment or at that thing. Then you failed. However, it does not mean that you were a failure. It means that version of you may have been a failure. Alternatively, it means that version of you failed to have a critical piece of information to succeed—a piece of information you now have from the failed attempt or failure; a piece of information you can now apply to the next version you choose to propel into the world.

It's the exact same as an iPhone. There was version 1. They put out the best phone they could with what knowledge they had. It was far from perfect and had much to be desired. After feedback was received, Apple didn't then tuck their tail, assume they were a failure, and never make another phone. They went back to the drawing board with the insights they now had to perfect the next version. For all you perfectionists of the world, this is the process of perfection you should pursue. You have to put something out into the world and let the people you made it for critique it to truly allow it to inch towards perfection.

This happens through the repeated release of newer versions of you. Every time, you release a version that you believe is the best you can do. In that relationship you lost, you aren't experiencing a structural failure, and you are unlovable; you're realizing that version of you failed, and you can now apply the lessons learned to try again and experience less failure over time by being better as a person in the next relationship. That career you lost doesn't mean you were incapable of that job; it meant that version of you needs to improve, and in doing so, you have all the potential to get an even better and more fulfilling career.

Every failed aspect of your life can and should be run through this level if possible. This is where winners play because those failures become the fuel for our success. Scary actions give winners an actual level of joy because with the possibility of failure comes the opportunity of insights to help us lower the chances of failing again the next time we try, while inevitably increasing our chances of success. If a failure is run through this level, there is always a silver lining, so there is no longer a debilitating fear of failure, just a sense of confidence to take action that grows in knowing it's not an "if" we'll succeed but "when." This is the key to your true success and sustained drive to keep getting up when the world knocks you down. It's a clear sense of knowing that every action is a great action even if it ends in a supposed failure because it's just getting the bad reps out of the way and inching you closer to an inevitable win.

Predictable Failure

The final stage of failure is **predictable failure**. This essentially means that any time you attempt something, you are expecting something to fail. This doesn't mean you give half effort in any way. In fact, you give full effort. You do this because you're trying to find the faults so you can fix them. It's like putting water into the bucket so you can find and plug the holes. You actually have fun putting things out into the world and trying new things because you get joy out of giving your full heart to something and not attaching your identity to the outcome. You know it's potentially going to fail. You just want to get to the failure faster because you know it leads you to success even faster.

This is genuinely where I love to live personally. At this point in my life, my identity is not tied to what I create; it's tied to my efforts to create. I strive to get the bad reps out of the way because I know they are a necessary step on the path to mastery. When I played in the NFL, I went out to practice every single day with the complete understanding that I was going to give every play my full effort and still make mistakes, watch them on film, fix them, and get them right faster.

Then I'd go into games and do the same. Too many people question their purpose because they lack the progress. They've failed often, and it starts to kill passion. Perfection is not the goal. Progress is. Progress cannot happen without failure along the journey to strengthen you for the times when you'll need that strength. This is why athletes seem to have a knack for handling hardships and failures better than most. We're bathed in failure on a daily basis and we have no choice but to create an understanding of how to learn from failure and press on without shutting down from fear. We learn how to use failures as fuel to improve ourselves and our capabilities to sustain our trajectory in the direction of our dreams. This intangible is not reserved for athletes, however. Any person can do this.

SUSTAIN EXTERNALLY: DRIVE, HIVE & THRIVE

Once you understand how to handle setbacks from an internal standpoint and sustain your progress, the next step is to understand the external aspects of sustaining your progress and creating a shift through consistency and momentum. This is where we focus on drive, hive, and thrive.

Drive

Drive is a bit of a double-edged sword because there are internal and external components. You need internal drive to make sure you are sustaining your initiative and passion to continue your pursuit of the goals you have set for yourself, and you also must ensure you are sustaining the actual direction and speed towards your goals. In order to measure your passion or drive, you simply need to do a self-passion check and answer two questions. Do you still wake up with passion to take action towards your goals? And do you still carry passion to see yourself experiencing the end result of those actions?

If you find yourself having no passion for either, then you need to go back to the See Phase and begin again. If you find yourself only having a passion for experiencing the end result and no passion to wake up each day, then you need to go back to the Shift Phase and make adjustments. If you find yourself passionate about the day-to-day journey to your dream, and you have passion for the life you will experience when you achieve it, then you have arrived at a beautiful place, my friend.

Drive from a direction standpoint is simply having a check-in to make sure you're still making headway in the desired direction. Sometimes we'll get deep down the road of a path and pop our heads up to unfortunately notice we went off road somewhere and need to correct our course. I recommend frequent checks or an accountability partner to maintain course without falling off track too long, or at all.

Now comes drive towards a destination. I personally believe the destinations we shoot for in life are not the actual destinations we're trying to arrive at in life. When the destination is the only focus, most people sadly just "endure" the day to day so they can reach that destination. Then, even if they do arrive at their goals, it's short lived because they don't sustain the actions necessary to maintain their levels of success. They eventually slide back downhill. This is a perfect example of someone not making an identity shift to achieve their goal, making it much harder and much more likely they'll fall from grace.

When you make an identity shift, you'll find it much easier to sustain success because it's who you are to do the hard things that attained that success in the first place. With this realization you'll find that the destination was never the destination. The destination was always the journey. The ability to wake up every day in a life you adore as you do the things necessary to achieve and sustain success with ease is what's important. Then, the destination is just the cherry on top, as you actually desire getting back to your day-to-day life that you love because simply living it fills you with joy and confidence from the fulfillment you get doing the things that bring you success in life.

When I look at people in my life who are successful and have joy, it is always because they identify as the person who does the things that bring them success. The actions never drain them. In fact, they fill them up. I find that happiness isn't something us humans find randomly while looking for it. I have the deepest sense of happy when I'm working on something, as do the most fulfilled people I know. It seems to be a human urge to create, and it's in the flow of building that people find fulfilment, purpose, and a sense of bliss. These people found out how to apply all that I have shared in this book to elevate their lives and enjoy it more as well. Unlike you, however, they didn't have this process to follow, so they ended up having to take the hard way to the same destination. I only know this because they're part of my hive.

Hive

The **hive** is the group of people you keep around your life, and building your hive is difficult but incredibly rewarding and worth the effort. A hive is built two ways—adding and subtracting people from life. I have made one distinct realization, however. It's hard to add people to your hive without first removing people taking up space inside of it. So, you need to remove those who diminish your ability to create and live a life that's as sweet as honey. The problem is that we as humans have a need to be in community. So the thought of not having close friends, even if they're unhealthy for us, scares us into sticking with people that don't serve our dreams.

If you can make the choice to take the leap and leave a group of people that are harmful, there's a simple and effective way to proceed. First, if you have no desire to keep someone in your life, or you do not believe they can improve, then simply have the hard conversation and remove them from your world. Quick is easiest. In this situation, it is usually just you who will benefit from the action.

If you do believe someone has the capabilities of improving to become a person you need in your hive, then you can do the following. Schedule a time to have a meeting with them. The meeting will not be an easy one, but it will be a necessary one. This meeting will give you both an opportunity to improve; you'll get space to grow and give them an opportunity to grow as well. In this meeting, you'll need to share your thoughts in the order, and specific way, I outline. You'll understand why.

I see everyone's life like a business. The business has goals it is in business to achieve. In order for the business to have success, the employees need to do their jobs. If their jobs weren't getting done, then you'd pull the employees into your office for a meeting and have a discussion. You'd let them know they're performing poorly and that they'd need to improve if they wanted to keep their job. You'd let them know that you want them to do well, which is why you're having this meeting. If you didn't, you would have just fired them. You'd tell them they need to improve in specific areas you'd outline, and if they didn't, you'd have no choice but to let them go.

You're like that business, and all the people in your life are in employed positions in your life. You can't have two people holding a one-person position, so you can't even hire someone for the job until you remove someone. So you can't add great people to your business until you remove poor-performing ones. You'll need to set up meetings with the people who matter most in your life but aren't showing up the way you need them to. In this meeting, you let them know where the business is heading and why. You share your dream and why you want to achieve it. You let them know the position you see them holding and what you need from them. You tell them what kind of support you need from them in order to help you achieve that goal.

You also let them know that they don't have to get better, it's their choice completely, but if they don't, then they'll know why you went in a different direction or didn't include them. This way you've put the ball completely in their court to decide whether or not they want to do what's needed to be part of your life. The best part is that with this option, you've now given both people a chance to improve. You're giving yourself a chance to improve because you're doing what's needed to create a hive to make your life sweeter by achieving your goals with the proper community support every human needs to succeed. You're also giving them a chance to improve because they have someone who's telling them insights about what they can do to be better and be part of something special. Your life.

Now, you are not a perfect human being, and someone not adhering to your needs does not mean they are less than in any way. This just means you're both being given a chance to be in a new space without potentially weighing each other down based on each person's specific needs at the moment. You have to be selfish when it comes to your heart and be discerning about those who consistently take space in it. Your life and dreams need a full cup to continuously pour out from. If you're going to make a shift, you need to have a cup that has an abundance. If someone isn't filling your cup, you can no longer pour into theirs. This isn't a mean action; it's a meaningful action that will be better for you both in the end.

Subtracting people from your life isn't an easy step, but it's a necessary one. Dealing with this issue using this business-like method alleviates the stress you may have when considering removing someone from your life. This way they make the choice to either improve or exit without you harboring any guilt. You get to press on and take care of adding to your hive.

While making additions to your hive will benefit you, it often takes just as much energy, and it can be just as uncomfortable, to find strangers and ask them to be a part of your life. Making additions to your hive means finding new friends or reaching out to colleagues you're only acquainted with or joining coaching groups and new communities. It means putting yourself out there and taking a chance at rejection or making a financial investment in these communities. It can also make you feel vulnerable to essentially be seen as someone in need. It's difficult to go out into the world and meet new people who may have accomplished more than you and ask to be a part of their life. If they're smart, they're also protecting their "business" of life. You have to add to their cup in order for them to pour into yours. If you feel like you have no value to give them, you'll assume you shouldn't even contact them.

This would be a mistake. You have many ways to add value to a person's life and you have to figure out what these are. You have to put yourself out there and share your heart and ideas. You have to show that you see your value, and then they will be able to see it. Again, these are all things that are scary, but adding people to your hive is necessary for you to thrive. It's how the greats became great. They were willing to join a group at the bottom and climb their way to the top. This only happens when you create the space in your life to add people and then actually add them.

You may find that the most promising path is making an actual financial investment into a group or community. Yes, you may have to pay to play. Does that trigger you? Well, I respectfully would like to press into that area. People pay money to put their kids into sports, starting as young as five years old. That's a community. People pay for their kids to go to colleges, and the better the college "community"—teachers, alumni, etc.—the more you pay. People pay to attend concerts and be in a community of people with similar interests. So why is it so odd for you to pay for a community that actually returns on that investment? This is why coaching, masterminds, etc., are such a smart thing. It's the community you put money out for that can bring money back to you through a business, a better career, or even a better relationship.

It can be painful to the ego to try and meet new higher-level people by putting yourself out there or by investing actual money into a community. The people who let their egos stop them end up sitting in the stands, watching others play the game of life together at a higher level. Get out of the stands, get onto a team, and get in the game.

Once you do, you'll give yourself the chance to truly thrive in life. When I consider success, I think about thriving at a higher level. It excites me because of the level of joy I know I can have when I give of the abundance I've earned. It genuinely fills me up, partially because I get to feel the experience of providing what I never had growing up from this side of the relationship and partially because I selfishly know it's going to provide me with clarity to stretch into my own higher levels of success.

Thrive

The **thrive** section is fairly easy to lean into. Seek service. That's it. Seek a location and level of service that creates a return of pride and joy that makes you desire more of that feeling. When you give, you actually get. You get to feel a feeling that's hard to put into words. A feeling that can, in fact, be expanded upon. A feeling you can have more of.

Once you realize that you can have more of it, you will start seeking the pathway to that happening. On that journey you will find a clear direction of what must be done. It will look like work. It will feel like a worried excitement. It will be you SEEing the next level for your life to lead into. It will restart this beautiful process of growth into the unlimited abundance waiting for you. You will see how you can enter into the next level of making an identity shift in your life.

REFLECTION SECTION

Shift a Failure – Where in your life can you shift the perspective on a failure from a negative light to a positive one to garner confidence and/or hope from it?

FriendShift – Where can you honestly say you need to remove a friend from your life and/or add someone who may be more beneficial in regard to achieving new levels of success?

Give a Shift – If you were thriving at the greatest level you can imagine, where would you give of your resources to help someone else succeed and why?

CHAPTER 9

SO, WHAT PROMISE...?

I want to leave you with the same question I shared earlier, which I ask every one of my guests on the *Aww Shift Podcast* www.AwwShift.com. I'm hoping that maybe you've given the question some thought at this point.

What promise did God make to the world when he created you?

And if you don't like how it's worded, then: What promise did your creator make to the world when you were created?

I didn't share this before, but I'm a man who will always give the credit where it's due. I can't actually take credit for this question. In the world of what I do, I happen across incredible hearts and minds. If I'm lucky, I get a chance to set aside time and have a chat with these people. One such person is a man named J.R. Reed.

We set aside some time to chat, and I was working in a Starbucks nearby my home at the time. When you get on the phone with people, it's usually just a bit of loose banter and basic questions to get a feel for where someone is, who they are, what they're about, etc. J.R. didn't feel like traversing the casual conversation stages with me and he went right for the jugular in his opening questions. "What promise did God make to the world when he created you?"

This guy stopped me dead in my tracks and left me stuck in thought. I'd never been asked this question before and I had zero clue how to answer it at that moment. Was I supposed to answer in a philosophical way? Was I supposed to answer in a logical, realistic manner? Should it be a lofty reason? I went directly into my head and I got scrambled in thought.

Over the years, I've come to find that the answer is less of something you go into your head to find and more of something you go into your heart to find. I believe you have a little voice in the background that is quietly telling you what the promise of your life to this world is. A little voice that's aching to be heard. This voice is actually yelling at the top of its lungs, but you're either living a life so loud with distractions and difficulty that you can't make it out or you're so fearful of what listening to and embracing this voice may mean you have to shift that you ignore it.

The next level of your life is one that should awaken something deep inside of you that finds a fire of inspiration, not simply from a possible accomplishment but from a possible "being." This place is in such powerful alignment with who you are and how you live that life itself makes you feel like exploding with joy. The next level of your life is one that should be born from that quiet voice you finally choose to listen to. The voice you come to hear by clearing the distractions and noise. By embracing the fear of what greatness may ask of you. By choosing the life you want to live because, for possibly the first time ever, you choose the person you want to become.

You no longer have to live to serve the beliefs and identity of a you that was created when you were a child by people not living your life. You no longer have to live in service to the desires of others but can finally live to the desires you have for your own life—the desires that your creator has for your life based on the seed planted deeply into your heart and mind well before you entered this world. A seed that is the source of that voice calling out to you from the void, begging you to live the life you were promised to live.

It's time for you to stop taking in insights and information just to let them sit idly in the back of your mind. You need to stop living a life of quiet survival. A life of settling for what you have because it's hard to upgrade to the next level. Hard is hard for a reason. Hard leads to happiness. Happiness from overcoming hard. A gift you can only receive by taking action on the path that heads in the direction of your dreams.

Embark on the path to your purpose and promise. The journey to get there leads directly down a path of an identity shift into the identity you want, and need, to be. The identity you are promised to this world to be. If you listen to your heart, I believe you may come to find they are one in the same.

My answer to JR's question at that time is different than it is now, not because the promise is actually different but because I am. I have chosen to listen to that voice and follow the words. The louder the voice gets, the clearer it gets about who I need to become to fully shift into my identity promised to this world. I am working the best I can, day in and day out, to keep that promise. It's time to upgrade how you operate and elevate your life. It's time to keep the promise God made to the world for your life.

As you continue down that path, I will as well. The journey to writing this book past all the hardships life has thrown at me has become one of my greatest joys. It's like a new child being put out into the world. The shifts I have made led me here and they have been some of the greatest, and most difficult, of my life. However, I wouldn't have it any other way. There are days I am just sitting in my home with my entire family all around me doing something as simple as eating dinner. An activity we never did growing up, as we would all just get our food and scatter to our corners of the house. It's in those family moments that I can most connect to what my shifts have given me.

My shifts in life gave me feelings I can't put into words, skillsets that give me power and control, friendships that make life a joy, and a purpose that makes life fulfilling. A purpose that I'm honored to live out every single day as I share my life and research in a manner that I believe helps people become better versions of themselves. The same way I helped Christine become a better version of herself despite the funky hole she somehow found herself in. The same way I helped Ken make a shift in his life and a commitment to being an entirely upgraded version of himself.

You don't remember Ken's transformation taking place this whole time? Ahhhhhh, well, that's most likely because you were busy reading and thinking about yourself. That's OK, though. It's expected. See, while you were reading, Ken was reading right along with you and applying everything he absorbed. He completed all of the exercises and was able to make an identity shift. Time in the "book world" moves a little bit faster than your time, so he's accomplished a lot. You know what? I think Christine and Ken have another breakfast scheduled right now. You want to peek in on them?

EPILOGUE

I've been here seven times and have never seen anyone order that bagel. It looks delicious. "Hey, miss, do you mind me asking how you had them prepare that bagel for you?"

"Oh," she chewed down the last bite before continuing to answer, "it's just toasted with a little bit of salmon cream cheese, avocado, and olive oil."

"Now why are you interrupting that woman and her breakfast, Ken? She's obviously trying to enjoy her meal."

The woman smiled, and I turned to greet my dear friend Christine with an even bigger smile. We locked eyes, and there was a light in hers that was different that the last time we'd connected over seven months ago. It was a light that came from what her face was telling me was pride and astonishment at how she now saw me.

She sat down in the reddish brown chair across from me that seemed to perfectly compliment the glowing purple dress and yellow shoes she chose to wear to our morning get together.

"Look at you, Ken! My heart just doubled in size seeing you and feeling the energy coming off of you. Not to mention that somehow you've beaten me here. How have you been?"

"Christine," I said and then paused while I took a deep and quickly exhaled, "I have been beyond great"

"Oh, have you? Do tell," she said as she shot me an "I told you so smile" and crossed her arms as she sat back in her chair fully prepared to listen in.

I left our last meeting a little sad and frustrated because I knew what you were saying was right, but my ego was definitely bruised. I sat on the conversation for a couple days and kept going through my same daily regimen and thinking process until one day something hit me. I started to extrapolate my life forward years from now and saw what it would look like if I kept doing the same things. The first realization was that I would lose our friendship, and that hurt to think about. Then I realized I would most likely be heavier, in more debt, and vastly more unhappy than I already was.

So I googled this Anthony Trucks guy and looked into some of his videos online. He seemed like a great guy and he actually happened to have a book out called *Identity Shift*. So I grabbed it on online and waited for it to arrive, knowing I was going to most likely be making some changes. While I was waiting for its arrival, I took it upon myself to simply start cleaning my house. I have no idea why, but the thought of a clean house when starting this journey to a better version of myself seemed like a great idea.

"Funny you say that, Ken. That's actually something he highly recommends when you want to clear the space for a new venture.

Start with your immediate environment to set the tone. I'm guessing you probably picked that up from one of his videos and subconsciously took action. That's great!"

"Thank you, Christina. It felt great. The anticipation of the book oddly started to build, and I found myself checking the delivery date frequently because I wanted to dig in. Simply knowing how his work had changed your life left me in eager anticipation to see what exactly it was that you did to make your shift."

"Look at you using the word 'shift.' Now I know you're a true Shift Starter." She grinned at me.

"Yes, I am. He's a great teacher, and I love the way he easily explains everything. When that book finally arrived, I dug in immediately. I loved the opening story in the first chapter also. Felt so familiar. As I started getting deeper into the book, one page at a time, my mind seemed to be expanding by the minute. His story was powerful, and his processes that I could apply to my life were just as impactful. I answered the reflection section questions. I downloaded the worksheets, and I completed everything in the book over the last seven months.

"Christine, I committed to the upgraded version of me and how I operated. Then, everything shifted. The way I chose to start my days every day gave me power, confidence, and an odd sense of purpose. The way I looked at myself in the mirror and the way I actually thought about how I was operating in every moment was a new and powerful feeling. I could actually start to see my identity as it was and how I wanted it to be in an ideal world. Understanding in key moments of my life how my mentality was processing information through the Life Mastery Loop and taking actions that would actually create my identity gave me a control I'd never thought was possible. I was able to see my roots and fruits in a different light, reframe my failure, and essentially reprogram my mind. I was able to change in ways I never thought possible."

"Wow, Ken. I'm genuinely speechless and so incredibly excited for you. So what have you created in your life since then?"

"Well, I start every day with an odd sense of joy because I feel like I'm getting closer to understanding the promise God made for my life to this world. I wake up early. I follow a beautiful morning routine that sets my emotional and mental tone for the day. I'm out the door early and in a great mood so nothing easily penetrates my joy or brings me down, even when people cut me off. The old, outdated me used to freak out when that happened! I've started working out more and have lost 17 pounds, and I feel lighter and happier in my own skin. I quit my job because I finally applied for the job I've wanted for so long and I got it!"

"Congrats, Ken! Look at you moving up in the world!"

"That's the crazy part though, Christine. I may have to quit it soon."

"Why's that?"

Well, I finally finished writing that book and self-published it. People from all over the world that I've never met before started reading and sharing it and asking if I can teach them how to do what I shared in the book. So that business I thought would be a side business, if I ever did launch it, is now making me as much money as my full-time job, and I'm only working six hours a week at it. It's genuinely unbelievable to see what my life looks like compared to what it looked like the last time we talked."

"You're telling me, Ken. I feel like I'm sitting with someone I've never met before. Have you experienced the downside of the shift yet?"

"Now I want to ask you, 'What downside?', but I know exactly what you're talking about. I have lost some friends who weren't a good fit for me anymore. They weren't too happy, and they had some choice words for me. It was the hardest part, but I know I planted some seeds and I hope they grow into shifts in their lives."

"I know exactly what that feels like."

"I know you do, Christine. To be honest, it's why I am so much more grateful for you than you know. You could have easily just cut me out and not given me the energy to show me how to upgrade my life. You could have left me to slither off and continue living my life the way I was. You didn't, though, and it's quite literally changed my life. I can't tell you how thankful I am that you showed up in my life the way you did, WHEN you did. I'm forever in your debt."

"No debt. All I ask is that you continue to pass it on. Anthony is all about leaving an impact on the world. As a Shift Starter I have made a commitment to changing my world so I can change the world, and it's the same commit I'm going to ask of you. Just pay it forward to the next people you see have the capabilities of making a shift and guide them to the work that can change their lives."

"There is zero doubt in my mind that I will do that. Sometimes I sit back and think about who I used to be just seven months ago, and it blows my mind because I can barely get back into the mind space of that guy. What he used to appreciate, what he used to make fun of, what he used to think was OK, and how he used to simply operate without even truly seeing himself."

"It is a crazy realization, but believe me, Ken, it gets so much better. The life you have ahead of you is bountiful and abundant in ways that haven't even come into your head space yet. You think you know, but you have no idea. You know how you can't quite get into the head space of your old self now? It will happen again. In this moment, you are in a mental space that will be an old head space at some point, which means you will expand even further as you continue to apply the Shift Method."

"You continue to blow my mind, Christine. I seriously only wanted to take up about 15 minutes of your time as promised and I'm thankful you met with me, even if for just a few minutes. I'm off to a day date with a new person I met, and I can't wait for you to meet her. We ran into each other at the airport a month ago and noticed we were both reading the same book. Turns out she has a Christine in her life named Sam. This guy Anthony Trucks is out here changing lives."

"That he is, Ken. That he is."

I got up and gave Christine a gigantic hug and headed out the door, leaving her in the chair, smiling at me with a look of warm satisfaction and admiration. As I was walking down the street, I felt a wave of a new emotion that I'd never experienced before: overwhelming joy and appreciation for everything I am, everything I have, and everything I will be in the future. I had to fight back a tear as I walked down the street the street. Grinning from ear to ear, I must have looked like a crazy person. I had, in fact, upgraded my life to a level I never even fathomed existed. I can only imagine what the next upgrade will look like. What I do know is that it will be greater than I can picture now. Which is exactly what I want for you. Yes, you, reading these words right now. The time is now for you to start your journey to your next level.